MIGRATIONS

BEYOND WORDS PUBLISHING, INC.

4443 NE Airport Road

Hillsboro, Oregon 97124-6074

503-693-8700

1-800-284-9673

Printed in the United States of America

Distributed to the book trade by Publishers Group West

This book is printed on recycled paper.

DESIGN *Principia Graphica*

PRINTING *Dynagraphics*

BINDING *Roswell Bookbinding*

ELECTRONIC PREPRESS *Exact Imaging*

EDITOR *Julie Livingston*

Other books in the EarthSong Collection:

The corporate mission of Beyond Words Publishing, Inc.:

"INSPIRE TO INTEGRITY"

Library of Congress Cataloging-in-Publication Data

Wolfe, Art.

   Migrations : wildlife in motion / photographs by Art Wolfe ; text

by Barbara Sleeper.

     p. cm.—(EarthSong collection)

   Includes bibliographical references (p.   ).

   ISBN 0-941831-98-1 : $60.00

   1. Animal migration—Pictorial works. 2. Animals—Pictorial

works. I. Sleeper, Barbara. II. Title. III. Series.

QL754.W65 1994

591.52'5—dc20   94-25473

                                  CIP

Photographs by

Art Wolfe

MIGRATIONS

Wildlife in Motion

Text by

Barbara Sleeper

BEYOND
WORDS
Publishing
I N C

Since my initial publication in 1978, I have photographed for thirteen books. Each has had a different theme. Each has stemmed from a different interest. For instance, my book on the owls of North America sprouted from an isolated experience when I photographed a young owl in a Seattle park. I was so taken with this owl, and so excited at seeing it closely, that from then on, I was drawn toward owls as a camera subject. Over a nine-year period, I developed *Owls: Their Life and Behavior*.

Light on the Land formed in much the same way. When I participated in Ultima Thule's 1984 Everest expedition, my interest in landscape photography was heightened, and I was inspired to develop a project around this theme. On my diverse travels around the world, I began to document austere, dramatically lit landscapes. It took me eight years to gather the body of work for *Light on the Land*, and along the way I encountered conditions from the chaotic to the sublime.

Interestingly enough, *Migrations* began before either *Owls* or *Light on the Land*. When I was an art student at the University of Washington, I was exposed to the work of Maurits Cornelis Escher in design class. More than any other artist, M. C. Escher has influenced my work and the manner in which I perceive positive and negative space. Utilizing the motif of animals, he incorporated fish and birds, reptiles and insects into brilliant stylistic designs; the fluid transformation of organic forms is at once mesmerizing and soothing. I decided that if I could emulate Escher's mosaics through photographs, I would—regardless of the results.

I have seen vast flocks of birds, thundering herds of animals, and fluttering swarms of insects, and I have photographed them in a multitude of ways. I have flown in helicopters, microlights, and airplanes, floated in boats and canoes, waded in murky caiman-infested waters, and snorkeled beneath the crystalline seas of the South Pacific—always with the intention of gaining a perspective on the pattern that was being created by the wildlife passing before me.

In pursuit of material for *Migrations*, I've overcome numerous photographic challenges. An excellent example of this effort is embodied by the photograph of scarlet ibis in Trinidad. During the day, the birds are scattered out on the tidal flats preying on the crustaceans that live in the shallow waters, and like clockwork, they fly into Caroni Swamp at sunset, returning to their roost trees. Because of Trinidad's proximity to the equator, the sun sets abruptly, and there is only a small window of photographic opportunity when the ibis arrive at their roost sites. To compound the difficulty of photographing these birds, their roost trees are mangroves growing in water. Therefore, I was forced to shoot from a boat. Earlier I had scouted the site and determined what my needs were going to be. For the shoot, I brought an 800mm telephoto lens, two tripods, and a small forest of poles to the site. My guide and I quickly sank the poles into the mud and roped the boat securely to them so that I had a fairly steady platform on which to stand the tripods needed to steady the camera for the long shutter speeds required. Ultimately it took four hours of work. As the sun plunged into the ocean, the ibis began to arrive in waves of fifteen to twenty birds each. By the time the light had waned, several hundred scarlet ibis were perched in the mangroves. Watching the light meter fall within the viewfinder, I had only fifteen minutes before it became too dark to take a picture. The average shutter speed was approximately one to two seconds, and the percentage of usable shots was correspondingly low—perhaps only 10 percent were ideal for publication.

Another demonstration of the lengths to which I would go to get a picture is manifested in the shot of the lesser flamingos in Kenya's Rift Valley. I had heard about a young French microlight pilot who had been commissioned by Amboseli National Park to do an aerial survey of the last unpoached rhinos within park boundaries. I asked to tag along with him, and he graciously agreed. Over the course of the next three or four days, we flew over Amboseli, enabling me to photograph herds of African elephants and buffalo at a fairly low angle. Photographing from a microlight is ideal because it is infinitely more maneuverable than an airplane or a helicopter—and certainly more quiet, making it much easier to approach a subject without disturbing it.

On the pilot's day off, we decided to take the microlight a hundred miles away to Lake Magadi to take aerial photographs of the flamingos that migrate among the lakes of the Rift Valley. Photographing these birds was as exhilarating as photographing elephants. We flew over vast congregations—at times dropping down into the midst of flying flocks. It was a great experience, and the photographic opportunities were seemingly limitless. However, there were hidden dangers. Flying amongst the birds was quite disorienting, and the results could have been disastrous had the pilot not concentrated on his relative position with the ground. When we flew over a calm lake, height and distance became very difficult to read, and at times we found ourselves dangerously close to the water. It is not unheard of for a microlight pilot to crash and die as the result of misjudgment of altitude, but in this adventure, the microlight pilot and I happily survived to fly and photograph another day.

It was not until I began photographing for *Migrations* in earnest that I realized the extent of human penetration into the wildest places on Earth. It is simply impossible for terrestrial wildlife to avoid civilization. For example, there are only a few isolated areas in North America where species such as elk and caribou can roam free. There has been a concerted effort to preserve the last remaining areas of elk migration in Wyoming, and the remoteness of Alaska's North Slope has somewhat buffered the range of caribou from the effects of humans, but these are the last remaining outposts. Birds comprise a great part of this book, because unlike large, land-bound animals, they are still able to follow their migratory routes. They have the distinct and obvious advantage of being able to fly over congested areas to reach their destinations. The rapidly diminishing habitat of all wildlife, restricting both their numbers and their mobility, compelled me to document them before they are sealed into reserves. It is this freedom of movement which artistically paces the pages of *Migrations*.

Art, as well as conservation, is a goal of this book. Over the years, as I reviewed the material, I often had to pass over photographs because in a picture of masses of animals invariably one would be wandering in the wrong direction, thereby disrupt-

ing the pattern I was trying to achieve. Today the ability to digitally alter this disruption is at hand. For the first time in *Migrations*, I have embraced this technology, taking the art of the camera to its limits. Since this is an art book and not a treatise on natural history, I find the use of digitalization perfectly acceptable, and in a small percentage of the photographs I have enhanced the patterns of animals much as a painter would do on a canvas.

In completing this work on *Migrations*, I have gained more than anything else a better understanding of how wildlife in its multitudes is at the mercy of humankind—how the fragile balance is torn between the urge for development and the need for conservation. I recently witnessed a characteristic struggle in my own state of Washington, where a proposed expansion of an airport would have destroyed wetland habitat that supports a million migrating shorebirds annually. Fortunately, local environmental groups banded together and fought successfully for the preservation of this critical area. The list of similar stories is long. Seven caves in the Midwest support 85 percent of the known population of the tiny Indiana bat. Had this not been brought to light, these caves would have been opened up for exploration, and the bat would have been lost to mankind forever. In Antarctica I have seen entire rookeries of penguins obliterated by oil spilled from a grounded ship.

Migrations incorporates everything that is important in nature photography today. Visually stimulating, mentally engaging, it pulls the reader into a swirling vortex of movement and mass. As you look through the following pages, enjoy the magnificent spectacles of nature, but also pause to understand the delicate thread on which these large populations are dangling. Whenever a choice is presented to you to support a regional, national, or international conservation organization, please take the step for preservation.

Art Wolfe

It was late June. The humid night air pulsed with frog calls. Most Jamaican natives and beach-weary tourists had long called it a night. Yet in the moonlight along a deserted stretch of Jamaican coastal road, an invasion of white crustaceans was quietly taking place. In what looked like a scene from a Japanese sci-fi film, some of the creatures were poised at the edge of the road, and others cast long shadows as they boldly sidestepped across the pavement, raised high on their eight legs. The sound of chitin tapping tarmac was audible in the darkness. I had stumbled upon, not a beach invasion of aliens, but Jamaica's large, feisty land crabs returning from their annual reproductive migration to the sea.

Meanwhile, in South Africa, another remarkable wildlife exodus was underway. Termites—sprouting wings for the occasion—had emerged from the ground in incredible numbers to launch into the air on dispersal flights. A veritable feeding frenzy resulted as predators, turned brazen with the protein explosion, abandoned their cover. By day, birds, toads, and lizards gulped down the insects on the ground while swallows nimbly caught them on the wing. At dusk, bats swooped after the airborne insect morsels as nocturnal rodents and reptiles continued the feast below.

Everywhere, it turns out, creatures big and small are on the move. Spiders balloon on silken threads, salt-marsh aphids float on the sea surface, rice leafhoppers hitch rides with southwesterly weather depressions from central China to Japan. Bar-headed geese have been spotted flying over India's Dehra Dun at 29,500 feet, and a Ruppell's griffon once collided with a plane at 37,000 feet. African antelope and zebra migrate between dry-season waterholes and rainy-season browse. And in the deep oceans, the world's great baleen whales swim thousands of miles each year between their warm-winter calving areas and remote polar feeding grounds.

Clam worms, native to the European coast, spend the cold months among algae and in rock crevices, but during summer, they "go planktonic," swimming far from shore to reproduce. Near the South Pacific islands of Fiji and Samoa, on the first day of the last quarter of the October-November moon—like clockwork—writhing masses of amorous palolo worms rise to the surface of the water in a reproductive frenzy.

In autumn, thousands of spiny lobsters—normally solitary and reclusive by day—line up to march during the day in parallel, single-file lines across shallow areas between Florida's east coast and the island of Bimini in the Bahamas. Their abrupt mass movement in tight tail-to-antennae formation is a phenomenon unique among benthic crustaceans

While fish eggs, larvae, and young passively drift with the ocean currents, adults actively swim against them to reach their breeding areas. Migratory cod and herring move into deep water in autumn, spawn in winter, and return to shallow water in the spring. Certain stocks of Chinook salmon migrate thousands of miles in the open Pacific Ocean and then swim 2,000 miles up the Yukon River to spawn and die within yards of their freshwater birthplace. In contrast, European eels spend most of their twenty-year life cycle in freshwater streams, but mate and die in the Sargasso sea.

WHAT IS MIGRATION? ....

Strictly defined, migration is the regular, seasonal movement of all or part of an animal population to and from a given area—usually between breeding and wintering grounds. More broadly, it is the movement of any organism from one habitat to another. For the most part, this movement is horizontal, from a few miles to several thousand miles—but migration can also be vertical.

Planktonic crustaceans such as krill and squid remain at great depths during the day, rising to mass in the upper waters at dusk. Certain mammals, insects, and birds migrate vertically on mountainsides, frequenting upper zones to produce young, then the foothills or plains to avoid harsh winter weather. Each spring, herds of female Tibetan antelope migrate north across Tibet's vast Chang Tang Reserve to remote calving grounds in the Kunlun Mountains. In autumn, small groups of mountain quail walk literally single file down the slopes of the Sierra Nevadas to warmer elevations. Even the parasitic filarial worm makes a nightly vertical migration—from the host's deep tissues to those just beneath the skin for easy transfer to night-biting mosquitoes—their intermediary hosts.

Animal migrations are as regular as the changing seasons and the ebb and flow of the tides. Each spring, horseshoe crabs emerge from the sea like prehistoric trilobites to pile up on the sandy beaches of the Atlantic coast to mate and lay their eggs. Ruddy turnstones nest on the soggy Arctic tundra during the summer, then head for southern beaches in the fall to fatten on crabs, worms, and insects. Male scarlet tanagers, bright red during the spring breeding season in North America, exchange their showcase plumage for cryptic green feathers in which to winter safely in the jungles of South America. And come spring, barn swallows returning to North America follow the northern advance of the 48-degree isotherm—the very temperature at which insects begin to warm up and fly.

SUPERIOR ATHLETIC PERFORMANCE

Migration often requires extraordinary athletic abilities. Arctic terns hold the long-distance record for birds, migrating more than 12,500 miles in just four or five flights from Iceland, northern Alaska, and Canada to Antarctica, stopping only periodically to eat and rest. It has been said that their annual 25,000-mile, pole-to-pole migration is limited less by their endurance than by the size of the planet.

Using radar, scientists at Swarthmore College tracked millions of migrating warblers and shorebirds flying from Nova Scotia and Cape Cod off the Atlantic coast to the South American mainland. Pushed by trade winds from the Sargasso sea, most flew the distance nonstop in about eighty-six hours—the longest nonstop journey made by small birds over water anywhere in the world.

Most remarkable is the migration of the tiny ruby-throated hummingbird found east of the Mississippi. During summer, they migrate as far north as Canada, in winter, as far south as Panama. To do this, many must make a nonstop, 500-mile flight across the Gulf of Mexico—an Olympian feat considering that these high-metabolic hummers usually need constant flower nectar to maintain wing beats of fifty to seventy-five strokes per second. Scientists have estimated that a pre-migration weight-gain of just two grams of fat provides the fuel necessary for these iridescent jewels to fly 800 miles.

Equally impressive, the one-ounce blackpoll warbler loses half its body weight during a four-day, 2,400-mile migration between Nova Scotia and South America. To researchers calculating flight energetics, this represents a fuel efficiency equal to 720,000 miles per gallon.

This movement of wildlife around the planet went largely unnoticed until the advent of modern technology. During this century, aided by high-tech equipment that extends human perception, we have finally begun to tune in to the animal world as never before—and what we have learned has been eye-opening, if not humbling.

"The great streamings of birds up and down the planet are some of the most precise choreography in nature," wrote Jake Page and Eugene Morton in their book, *Lords of the Air*, "and to participate in them, even as a momentary observer, is to rise for a moment at least beyond the confines of one's own imagination, to imagine senses beyond ours . . . ."

By paying more attention to wildlife in motion, by witnessing ancient cranes dance and bow on their life-sustaining wetlands, by listening to the melodious underwater songs of humpback whales and the deafening, wing-flapping explosion of a million blackbirds erupting from their winter roosts, by watching penguins glee-fully toboggan over the Antarctic ice fields, and by discovering the migration routes of animals crisscrossing the planet, we have finally begun to learn more about our own part in this global equation. Life-forms one and all, we are as intricately woven into the ecological tapestry as an armadillo or a slime mold.

The perpetual movement of wildlife over the planet is driven by a positive energy force that transcends time to link us as much to the extinct dinosaurs as to a formation of geese flying overhead. Animals, including people, initiate pilgrimages in order to find food, exploit seasonal resources, seek warmth, or find adequate space to establish territories, mate, and raise young. These migrations are often triggered by an interplay of environmental factors—food availability, weather conditions, day length, even the phases of the moon—coupled with subtle directives from an animal's endocrine glands, such as the pituitary, that influence both reproductive development and metabolic rate. Whatever the reason, we all move to survive—because life *is motion*.

HOW DO THEY DO IT?

We've come a long way since Aristotle thought that swallows hibernated in the mud and others believed that birds flew off to the moon each fall. In an effort to study animal movements, ingenious marking techniques have been implemented in order to keep tabs on mobile subjects. Boat-propeller scars on manatees have been photographed and computer-catalogued; butterflies have been sprayed with harmless dyes; numbers have been painted or scratched on tortoise, crab, and snail shells; disks or clips have been attached to the fins of fish and the ears of large mammals; numbered and color-coded tags, rings, or bands have been attached to the legs or wings of birds and bats; stainless-steel pins have been fired into whales; harmless radioactive chemicals have been fed or injected into animals, causing their scats to "glow"; and nocturnal animals have been dusted with fluorescent powders.

To unravel the overwintering migration mystery of the eastern monarch, adhesive price-tag labels were squeezed onto the wings of hundreds of thousands of butterflies. As individual tagged specimens were returned over many years, their migration route eventually began to appear in a trail of map pins from Canada to Mexico.

Radar has been used to track bird and insect movements, and sonar to track fish. Now, space-age technology, using microminiaturized transmitters bouncing signals via satellite to computers, is making it possible to track far-ranging animals such as sea turtles, peregrine falcons, whales, and sharks to remote corners of the Earth.

In spite of improved efforts to learn where animals go, how they navigate still remains shrouded in mystery. Most have an uncanny map sense and appear guided as if by built-in compass. When a manx shearwater was experimentally removed from a British nesting colony and released in Boston, it returned to its island burrow among thousands in just twelve and a half days—after flying 3,000 miles across the Atlantic from a starting point unknown to it. Such navigational feats underscore the fact that animals have sensory perceptions far superior to our own.

For starters, pigeons can "see" ultraviolet light and hear low-frequency sounds generated thousands of miles away by landforms such as mountain chains, which actually emit their own infrasonic signatures. Fish not only can hear and smell, but many generate their own electric fields for navigation through murky water. The desert ant has a thousand lenses to our one—eighty specially adapted for receiving polarized light. Recently, biologists painstakingly proved that ants plot compass direction using polarized light patterns from the sky—and that they may reckon distance by actually counting their tiny steps.

Some birds migrate by day, others at night. By aiming telescopes at the moon, it was discovered that most nocturnal flights occur from shortly after dark until midnight. Night fliers appear to navigate by the position of the stars, and daytime fliers by the sun—possibly with the aid of the Earth's magnetic field on overcast days. Birds also seem to have an internal clock that helps them compensate for the sun's changing position. Similar mechanisms have been proposed for some insects, crustaceans, and fish.

Not only does migration call for extraordinary feats of navigation and endurance, but it can be dangerous. A large number of migrating birds do not live to see the spring. Predators and human hunters eliminate some. Floodlit towers and smokestacks lure thousands more to their deaths. Mortality rates are especially high for the young attempting their first migration. Winds can blow birds off course, and bad weather can throw off their fuel and energy budgets. Feathers of small birds found in the stomachs of deep-sea fish attest to the annual loss of sea-crossing migrants. In foul weather, birds often drop from the sky to cling to a ship's rigging or to expire on the decks. Tired travelers fare slightly better over land, where they can stop and rest. Knowing this, avid bird watchers stock their backyards with birdseed and stake out cemeteries, city parks, and garbage dumps in hopes of adding migrant species to their life lists.

And for many animals on the move, timing is everything—with little room for error. Arrive in the Arctic too early, and snow cover, lack of food, and cold temperatures can eliminate the possibility of breeding. Arrive too late, and food may run out and the weather deteriorate before the young are fledged. When quality of territory is a factor in mate acquisition and reproductive success, males must arrive early enough to stake out a good one, but not so early as to weaken, leaving them unable to defend their precious terrain against stronger, later-arriving males.

GLOBAL ARTERIES OF LIFE

The loss of migration corridors, breeding grounds, and critical refueling stops along traditional migration routes is undoubtedly the biggest threat to wildlife on the move. Many of Africa's great herds of migratory animals—wildebeest, springbok, eland, and zebra—have disappeared along with their migration routes. In Botswana, fences erected to restrict the spread of hoof-and-mouth disease among cattle also prevent migrating antelope herds from reaching their traditional watering places, causing millions to die during drought.

Wetlands are especially important to migratory species. From ethereal swamps, cranberry bogs, and cattail marshes to the Everglades' "river of grass" and the soggy Arctic tundra, these waterlogged lands are crucial refuges for fish, birds, and other wildlife. Yet the Atlantic flyway lost half of its coastal wetlands in just thirty-five years.

With habitat destruction occurring at such alarming rates, scientists are hard-pressed to learn more about the critical habitat requirements—and often secret overwintering areas—of species before these areas are lost. More than 350 species of birds breed in North America but migrate south to winter in either the Caribbean Islands, Mexico, or Central and South America. These Neotropical migrants are highly vulnerable to habitat changes at both breeding and overwintering sites as well as along their migration routes.

The broader implications of animal movement over the planet should not be overlooked. Migratory species make a political statement. When birds fly from state to state, from public to private land, and from nation to nation, they remind us that we are all members of a larger global community. Clearcut a rain forest in Venezuela and it can affect bird populations in New York. As we continue to unravel the mysteries of migration, one thing is clear: From farmer to forester, from politician to scientist, we all need to cooperate to protect these precious global arteries of life. Ultimately, their preservation will require interstate and international cooperation.

Most important, by learning more about the sensory perceptions and ecological requirements that make such magical journeys possible, not only do we share in the sheer wonder and exuberance of life on planet Earth, but we gain invaluable insights into the environmental prerequisites for our own survival. By monitoring the vitality of migratory species, we, in turn, measure our own.

Barbara Sleeper

¹ ADÉLIE PENGUINS *Pygoscelis adeliae*

Amboseli National Park, Kenya

Loxodonta africana AFRICAN ELEPHANTS [2]

—

4   AFRICAN OPENBILLS *Anastomus lamelligerus*

The Everglades, Florida

5 AMERICAN ALLIGATORS *Alligator mississippiensis*

Adélie penguins have been aptly compared to champagne corks, as they pop eight feet straight up out of the water to land on icebergs or rock ledges. And they seem almost gleeful as they jump and belly glide off ice walls back into the water. While relegated to clumsy waddling and hopping on land, penguins are beautifully designed for energy-efficient swimming and diving. Using their featherless, leathery wings for propulsion, they literally fly underwater at speeds of twenty miles per hour or more. Hydrodynamically shaped like flying ovals, with their heads tucked into their shoulders and webbed feet held straight back to steer, penguins transform underwater into high-speed avian torpedoes. Thick down, waterproof outer feathers, and layers of fat protect these aquatic gymnasts from the cold, and solid bones serve as ballast for dives as deep as 850 feet. Porpoising at the surface to breath like tiny dolphins, they also add a lubricating coat of air bubbles to their body surface which helps reduce frictional drag. Except when they come ashore to breed, penguins spend most of their time at sea, flying underwater to feed on fish and krill.

Life would be idyllic for the Adélies if not for the meat-eating leopard seals that patrol their rookery shoreline. Hunting solo, the predatory seals hide beneath ice floes waiting for penguins to plop into the water. They also single out birds as they return to the rookery. Once a target is spotted, the large seal drops beneath the surface to ambush its prey from below. Leopard seals can swim faster than penguins and will pursue their intended victim over and under ice floes until the bird eventually tires. Then, like skinning a grape, the seal grabs the bird by its feet, and with a violent snap of its head, rips the penguin right out of its skin. Each nesting season, leopard seals kill an estimated 5 percent of the Adélies' breeding population.

African elephants once migrated over much of the Dark Continent. Now these living relics are restricted to national parks and other habitat islands surrounded by encroaching humanity. Adult males stand ten feet high at the shoulders and weigh close to six tons. Yet despite their size as the planet's heaviest land animal, elephants walk almost silently through the vegetation on their enormous cushioned feet. This ability, coupled with their coloring—dust-covered by day and black at night—allows these giants to move through the landscape almost undetected. At night, it's easier to walk into an elephant than to see one. By day, they spend considerable time browsing. Their feeding habits are quite destructive, as they routinely topple large trees just to nibble a few leaves at the top. Restricted to shrinking habitat areas that allow no exit for the elephants and no chance for the vegetation to regenerate, the elephants will eventually destroy their own habitat—a habitat also needed by other wildlife. In parks where this is a problem, elephant population control measures have been initiated. In other areas, such as Zambia's Luangwa Valley National Park, this hasn't been necessary. Once called the "Valley of Elephants," the Luangwa Valley was famous for its large herds. In just a few years, 80 percent of the elephants were killed by poachers wielding automatic rifles.

Depending on the quality of their habitat, elephants can spend up to eighteen hours a day feeding. They manipulate their food with their trunks—the longest animal noses in the world. A combination of upper lip and nose, the trunk can be used for grabbing and smelling at the same time. The African elephant has two "fingers" at the tip of its trunk which it uses to grab small objects. More than 40,000 muscles and tendons in the trunk enable an elephant to pick up a peanut or to lift a heavy log. Thousands of migratory elephants congregate in Botswana's Okavango Delta each year. Often, when crossing the deep-water channels, only the tips of their trunks are visible above the surface of the water, serving as handy pachyderm snorkels.

The namesake open space in the center of their large bills as well as their brownish-black plumage help identify these distinctive birds as African openbills. Their sailing flight with rounded tail and long dangling legs are also clues. Openbills feed by wading in still water, often submerging their heads completely under the surface to search for freshwater mussels—their preferred food. In fact, their gaping bills are a special adaptation to their mollusk diet. Like gourmet chefs, these members of the stork family prepare the mussels in several different ways. Some crush and remove the shells of the mussels underwater before swallowing them, others gulp them down shell and all. Those who are more patient carry the mussels to dry land where they let the hot sun bake them open before eating them. If given the opportunity, openbills will also eat crabs, fish, and frogs.

There are only two living species of alligators in the world: the American alligator and the rare Chinese alligator found in the freshwater marshes along the Yangtze River. The American alligator is an impressive beast possessing spiked scales, powerful legs, a strong tail, and clawed feet. With most of its body concealed underwater, an alligator's size is deceptive. While the record length for an American alligator is nineteen feet, two inches, most adults average ten to twelve feet in length. Some can weigh a hefty 600 pounds or more.

Agile swimmers, these archaic reptiles tuck their legs close to their sides and propel their bodies forward with graceful sidestrokes of their muscular tails. These flattened, oarlike tails allow for serpentine gliding and also enable alligators to leap out of the water with incredible speed. Like reptilian submarines, they can float at the surface like nondescript logs, then sink ominously out of sight, leaving only a telltale stream of bubbles. Alligators can hold their breath for more than forty-five minutes. And in spite of appearances, they are no slouches on land. In addition to lethargic waddles and belly glides off banks, alligators can run faster than people over short distances by rising up on their hind legs in a "high walk" that is as startling as it is fast. During the dry season, alligators often cover great distances on land in search of water.

Mycteria americana AMERICAN WOOD STORKS **7**

6 ANCIENT BUSHMEN ROCK CARVINGS

Twyfelfonstein region, West Central Namibia

8 BALD EAGLES *Haliaeetus leucocephalus*

Southeast Alaska

9 BAT STARS *Patiria miniata*

Queen Charlotte Islands, British Columbia, Canada

Most hunter-gatherer societies, such as that of the Bushmen of the Kalahari Desert, lived in perfect harmony with nature, following ancient ways that protected their natural resources. Like the wildlife populations around them, the size of the Bushmen bands was limited to the number of people a territory could support without straining the ecosystem. So skilled were the Bushmen at managing their replenishable resources, having an extensive knowledge of roughly 200 species of plants, that Bushmen bands could live in areas of the Central Kalahari where no water is available 300 days of the year.

According to South African writer Alf Wannenburgh, who lived with the Bushmen for several months, "They speak of their origins, not in terms of historical tradition, but in reference to a mythical time when all animals were people like themselves, speaking the same language." Wannenburgh described how the members of a Bushmen hunting party could interpret every mark left in the sand by a giraffe and how they even seemed to anticipate its moves before they finally killed it with poisoned darts. Because the Bushmen believe that animals were once human, the wanton slaughter of animals is considered taboo. Killing an animal is acceptable only in cases of self-defense and for food. Today, the traditional ways of the Bushmen are as endangered as the wildlife they once hunted. "The ancient bond between the Bushmen and the land has now all but disappeared," says Wannenburgh, "and with it the mutually preserving relationship between hunter and prey."

Wood storks are tactile feeders. With the tips of their open bills submerged in the water, they literally feel for their prey, gulping down anything that moves, including snakes, frogs, fish, and young alligators. The bare skin on a wood stork's head and neck has led to some unflattering nicknames: flinthead, ironhead, hammerhead, gourdhead, and Spanish buzzard. Formerly called the wood ibis, they are the only species of stork to nest in North America. Wood storks stand three and a half feet tall and have a wingspan of five feet. Like cranes and ibis, wood storks fly with necks extended and long stiltlike legs outstretched behind. Flocks sometimes fly in circles and ascend to tremendous heights, alternately flapping and soaring in unison high over the cypress swamps, suddenly to descend—or to soar out of sight.

Wood storks once nested along the Atlantic and Gulf coasts from South Carolina to Texas from November through April. At the turn of the century, 150,000 wood storks inhabited Florida. Today, this steadily declining species is limited primarily to peninsular Florida. Many of the tall cypress trees in which they nest have been logged for timber. Drainage, droughts, and a dropping water table have gradually dried up their feeding areas. It is the seasonal increase in available food—when fish congregate in dry-season waterholes—that normally triggers their reproductive cycle. Wood storks will not assemble, or breed, if there is an inadequate supply of fish. The reason is based on wood-stork economics. In the fifty-five days that their three to four chicks are in the nest, each requires roughly fifty pounds of fish before they are old enough to fledge. The disappearance of 95 percent of the water birds from Florida's Everglades is an indication of the damage that has been done to this fragile ecosystem.

Both in legend and symbolism, bald eagles figure prominently in Native American cultures. According to Haida legend, the bald eagle is Chief of the Sky Beings. Zuni Indians carve stone fetishes to pay homage to the Eagle, Hunter God of the Upper Regions. In keeping with this tradition, the majestic bald eagle was also chosen as the national symbol of the United States. These fierce-eyed predators once bred throughout North America. Habitat loss, pesticide poisoning, and poaching subsequently endangered the white-headed eagles in all the lower forty-eight states except Washington, Oregon, Minnesota, Wisconsin, and Michigan, where they are considered threatened.

For years, field research has been conducted on local animal populations using radio telemetry. In a landmark study conducted in 1984, scientists at the Army Research and Development Office at the Aberdeen Proving Grounds in Maryland tracked the movements of a bald eagle using satellite telemetry. Researchers attached a specially-designed transmitter pack to a bald eagle. Signals from the transmitter were received by Argos DCLS instruments aboard two Tiros-series weather satellites on polar orbits. The signals were then transmitted to ground telemetry stations and relayed via commercial communications systems to processing facilities in Suitland, Maryland. From there the information was isolated and forwarded to Argos data-processing centers in Landover, Maryland, and Toulouse, France. It was then made available to the scientists via computer, telex, telephone, and other data-transmission networks. In all, it took between thirty minutes and three hours to transmit a message from the eagle to the scientists via satellite and ground links.

During the 244 days that the transmitter functioned, it provided one location fix per day on the bald eagle. To the surprise of everyone involved, the eagle flew from the Chesapeake Bay area to central Pennsylvania, then south to northern Florida, then north to the James River region of Virginia, and then on to North Carolina, returning within kilometers to its birthplace and the site where it had first been banded. The groundbreaking results were the first indication that a migrating bald eagle does not travel a straight route between two points. The study also provided the first look at how far a migrating bald eagle flies in a day and which habitats it uses during migration.

Today, satellite telemetry is making it possible to learn about the daily movements, migration patterns, and critical habitats of remote wildlife around the world. In fact, as this is being written, a satellite circling the cold vacuum of space is picking up signals from migrating caribou in North America, elephants in Africa, narwhals in Greenland, and migrating whales in the Pacific. By revealing the previously unknown migration paths of numerous wildlife species, space-age technology is now giving animals a "voice" in their own management and conservation.

BAT STARS *Patiria miniata* .... Queen Charlotte Islands, British Columbia, Canada

The rocky shores along the outer coast of the Queen Charlotte Islands are a magical place. Not only are they home to colorful bat stars that bejewel tide pools in rainbow hues, but maroon and orange sea cucumbers, red-tentacled tube worms, and sea anemones with scarlet stalks are found here as well. Enchanting underwater forests of bull kelp can grow up to eighteen inches a day. Held afloat by gas-filled bladders, the kelp's towering fifteen-foot blades sway gently in the currents as they reach for surface sunlight. In both color and beauty, the rich marine life found along these shores easily rivals that of a coral reef.

Several elements combine to make this abundance of marine life possible. The magnificent coastal forests can receive 200 inches of rainfall a year—making them one of the wettest places on Earth. The rugged, picturesque coastline, one of the highest wave-energy areas in the world, is pounded by enormous wind-driven swells

that are pushed across the Pacific. Each crashing breaker mixes plenty of air into the water, and marine life thrives with the abundant oxygen. Wind, warm surface water, and cooler upwellings then stir the nitrates and phosphates generated from decomposition into the broth. Mesmerizing tide-pool worlds are formed, filled with sea slugs, sculpins, snails, and chitons—and a galaxy of sea stars.

Called bat stars, or "sea bats," because of their webbed rays, these omnivorous, scavenging starfish feed by extending their voluminous stomachs over a variety of sessile or dead plants and animals. Their habit of readily extruding their sexual products—ripe sperm and eggs—when laid out on wet seaweed has made them a popular subject for embryological research. When the sperm and eggs are combined in sterile petri dishes, motile embryos develop overnight and grow into minute larvae which swim by vibrating their cilia.

10　BELUGA WHALES *Delphinapterus leucas*

Somerset Island, Canadian Arctic

'' ROCKHOPPER PENGUINS *Eudyptes chrysocome*

BLACK-BROWED ALBATROSS *Diomedea melanophrys*

Falkland Islands

Himantopus mexicanus BLACK-NECKED STILTS **12**

Llanos Plains, Venezuela

13   BURCHELL'S ZEBRAS *Equus burchelli*

Etosha National Park, Namibia

Amboseli National Park, Kenya

Syncerus caffer caffer CAPE BUFFALO **14**

From June to September, beluga whales congregate by the hundreds and thousands at the traditional breeding estuaries where they give birth. These ten- to sixteen-foot-long whales are unusual in the whale family because of their white coloration, well-defined necks, and ability to make a variety of agile body movements and facial expressions. Belugas have remarkable control of their bodies, using their flippers to swim in reverse, glide within inches of objects, and literally "stop on a dime." Their Latin name, *Delphinapterus*, which means "dolphin without a wing," refers to the fact that these smooth-backed whales lack true dorsal fins. Highly vocal, belugas moo, chirp, clang, clap their jaws, and whistle so loudly that at times their loquacious vocalizations can be heard above water—which explains why they have been affectionately dubbed "sea canaries." While feeding on schooling fish, belugas work closely together in small groups, forcing the fish into shallow water where they are more easily caught. To dislodge prey from the bottom, the white whales use suction and carefully aimed jets of water. Newborn belugas are camouflaged in brown, lightening to gray and then to white as they mature. Suckling for up to two years, the young whales remain close to their mothers during this time.

Albatross are the largest of all tube-nosed seabirds. The black-browed albatross glide on stiff outstretched wings that measure seven to eight feet across. Because they weigh nearly nine pounds and their legs are rather short, albatross usually take off on land or water by running into the wind or by simply dropping off a cliff into the air. Their long wings, their ability to drink salt water, and their diet of small seabirds and fresh seafood make it possible for albatross to ride the winds of the world's oceans for months at a time. They need to be on land only to breed, at which time they head for remote, uninhabited oceanic islands, where monogamous pairs perform elaborate courtship displays.

The black-browed albatross, named for the black line running through and over its eyes, is the most abundant of the albatross species found from the Antarctic to the Tropic of Capricorn in the Southern Hemisphere. Fearless at sea, they can often be seen closely following ships in pursuit of tossed garbage. Because of this trait, they were easily caught by European sailors in the nineteenth century who baited barbless hooks with fat. Black-browed albatross nest on ice-free oceanic islands during the summer months. They fill the air with cacophonous calls as they compete with each other for space. Mated pairs build cuplike, foot-high nests out of mud and grasses, and both parents incubate the single egg. It takes their chick nearly four months to mature. During that time, the chick is almost helpless—except for one defense. Should a skua or other bird of prey come too close, it will be hit with a fishy blast of projectile vomit.

Rockhopper penguins, adorned with decorative yellow or orange head plumes, are the smallest and most widespread of the six species of crested penguins. Millions of them live on the Falkland Islands, millions more on islands in the southern Indian Ocean. Nesting in huge noisy colonies, the birds seem to bicker and bray constantly. They are called rockhoppers because of their habit of bouncing from one rock to another as they travel about the boulder-strewn islands where they nest. Unlike many of the other penguin species, rockhoppers also jump into the water feet-first.

These large, graceful shorebirds are aptly named for their striking black-and-white plumage. Black-necked stilts walk along the shallow muddy borders of alkaline lakes and around freshwater wetlands on extremely long pink legs with graceful strides that can quicken to a run. Stilts have the longest legs in proportion to their body size of any bird except the flamingo. They use their needle-thin, needle-straight bills to probe for a diet of insects, crayfish, and snails. Widely distributed, black-necked stilts are found in southern and western North America, the Hawaiian Islands, the West Indies, Central America, and much of South America. The best way to observe shorebirds such as these is from a beachside road at high tide. Just as the tide begins to ebb, the birds start to actively feed, following the receding water.

Zebras are the only striped members of the horse family. As with human fingerprints, it is impossible to find two zebras with identical stripes. In fact, there is such a wide variation in pattern that some zebras are black with white stripes, and some even appear spotted. Their beautiful markings, however, have imperiled the species, as many are poached for their dramatic hides. Zebras are highly social, vocal animals that bray and bark to each other. They usually live in herds of five to twenty-five animals, typically females with young led by a stallion. During the dry season, zebras congregate in herds of a hundred or more and are often found in association with wildebeest. Their frequent need for water keeps them in close proximity to drinking holes.

Cape buffalo are armed and dangerous. Both sexes sport massive curved horns which sit atop their heads like Viking helmets. They can be deadly when aimed at predators or people. Cape buffalo are actually wild cattle. When alarmed, they produce an explosive snort, then raise their heads high looking for danger. Sounding such an alarm usually brings the entire herd to the defense of the frightened animal. So effective is this system of group defense that even blind and lame buffalo have been able to survive within the herd. Weighing up to 1,800 pounds, Cape buffalo can be especially dangerous if wounded or cornered. Hunters have reported numerous incidents of injured buffalo seeking revenge through ambush, circling through the undergrowth to charge the next person who passes.

Cape buffalo form cohesive herds that vary in size from a few animals to a thousand or more. If not in small bachelor herds, bulls can be solitary. During the rut, the heavyweight males frequently grunt, bellow, and clash. Such combat often results in serious injury. Adding to their rogue appearance, the bulls are usually caked in mud, which dries to form a protective coat against insect bites and excessive solar radiation.

Cape Cross, Namibia

15 CAPE FUR SEALS *Arctocephalus pusillus*

Cape Cross, Namibia

Brooks Range, Alaska

Rangifer tarandus CARIBOU **18**

17 CHINSTRAP PENGUINS *Pygoscelis antarctica*

South Georgia Island

19   CREVALLE JACK FISH *Caranx hippos*

20 ELEGANT TERNS *Sterna elegans*

Isla de Rasa, Mexico

An enormous Cape fur seal colony sits in the middle of a geographic paradox. On one side is a blinding, sun-baked desert with wind-whipped sand dunes towering as high as 800 feet—the world's highest—overshadowed by the 6,000-foot-high Naukluft Mountains. On the other side is the South Atlantic Ocean, teeming with marine life. How can such a stark desert extend right to the edge of the sea? The cold Benguela Current holds part of the secret. When the warm South Atlantic trade winds meet the cold water, a temperature inversion occurs, trapping a layer of cold moist air under a layer of warm air, which produces sea mist. Winds blowing parallel to the shore then hold this fringe of fog along the coastline, reducing the possibility of rainfall. The result is a shoreline devoid of vegetation and sparsely populated by desert-adapted spiders, insects, reptiles, sea birds—and the Cape fur seals. Black-backed jackals and brown hyenas occasionally patrol the beaches for fish at night. So effective has the cold Benguela Current been at keeping the rain clouds away that Africa's Namibian shoreline has earned the infamous title of "The Skeleton Coast."

Cape fur seals haul out of the cold South Atlantic by the thousands to bask and bark at the edge of Namibia's "Great Dune Sea." They are found along the sandy, rocky shores of southwest Africa and Cape Province from Cape Cross south to the Cape of Good Hope and east to Birds Island in Algoa Bay. Their colonies echo with a perpetual chorus of snorting and bellowing. These brown-coated seals are active by day, entering the water to chase fish. At night they sleep on shore, safe from attack by sharks and killer whales. Underwater, seals have superior vision, but on land they are nearsighted and are able to detect only motion.

Toward the end of October, the largest bulls begin to establish breeding territories on shore, threatening and fighting other males to defend them. Females group in harems of variable size on the male territories and give birth to single pups sired the previous year. Females come into estrus within a week after giving birth, yet once mated, they are able to delay implantation of the embryo until March or April. This adaptive strategy enables them to take care of breeding and birthing in the same season. Then the males and the females with young live apart until the breeding season begins again.

Chinstrap penguins perform a dramatic territorial display with wings extended and heads pointed skyward. So positioned, the namesake black band of feathers beneath their beaks becomes visible. When one calls, it often triggers a chain reaction among members of the rookery as others nearby join in to produce a raucous chorus.

Chinstrap penguins nest near the northern tip of the Antarctic Peninsula and on islands to the north, building their nests with stones. Even though their rookeries are usually near pebble beaches, they delight in stealing stones from their neighbors' nests. This pebble thievery seems to be a normal part of life in a chinstrap colony.

Caribou are circumpolar. They can be found in almost every direction around the North Pole, from Siberia and Scandinavia to Alaska, Canada, and Greenland. In North America, caribou migrate long distances between their winter and summer ranges—often as much as 800 miles. It is thought that they walk farther than any other animal, their passage accentuated by the incessant clicking of their snow-adapted hooves. Each winter, large herds migrate several hundred miles south from the Arctic tundra in search of food. Should they come to a river, they can swim up to six miles per hour. Woodland caribou and reindeer are essentially the same animal. The Micmac Indians of Canada called them *xalibu*, or "the one that paws." As a source of food, hides, and even transportation, these roving ruminants have long been a valued resource. In northern Finland, the Lapp people keep domesticated reindeer, drinking their milk and eating their meat. Many Lapps still use reindeer to pull their sleighs, and they fashion caribou hides into clothing.

In the fall, crevalle jack fish head for Florida's Crystal River, where the spring-fed water is warmer than the winter-chilled currents of the Gulf of Mexico. Thought to occur in most tropical and subtropical waters, jack fish can get quite large, weighing thirty-five to forty-five pounds. A record fifty-five-pound crevalle was caught at Lake Worth, Florida. Crevalle are common along the southeast coast of Florida and down through the Keys. Bright silvery fish such as these typically inhabit the well-lit surface waters of the ocean and the inshore waters of lakes. Flashing light off their silvery scales as if from a thousand mirrors, their shimmering color helps to camouflage them in the bright surface light and to confuse predators, making it difficult for them to pick out individual targets. The importance of this adaptation for survival is indicated by the many species of fish that protect themselves this way. When salmon and sea-run trout move from streams into lakes and oceans, they, too, turn silver.

If people drink sea water, they become more thirsty, dehydrate, and eventually die. The reason is because our kidneys need additional fresh water in order to eliminate the excess salt, and get it by desiccating body tissues and organs. In order to survive, birds also must limit the concentration of salt in their blood and body fluids to about 1 percent—less than a third the concentration of salt found in sea water. Elegant terns, like all seabirds, ingest large amounts of salt in their food and drinking water, yet they avoid dehydration. Their survival secret lies in the two salt glands positioned near their eye sockets. The glands draw excess salt from the bird's circulatory system to produce a fluid with a concentration of salt higher than sea water. Petrels forcibly shoot this saline liquid out of their tubular nostrils, whereas in most seabirds it just dribbles out. This explains why vigorous head-shaking is so characteristic of seabirds—they are literally shaking away their excess salt.

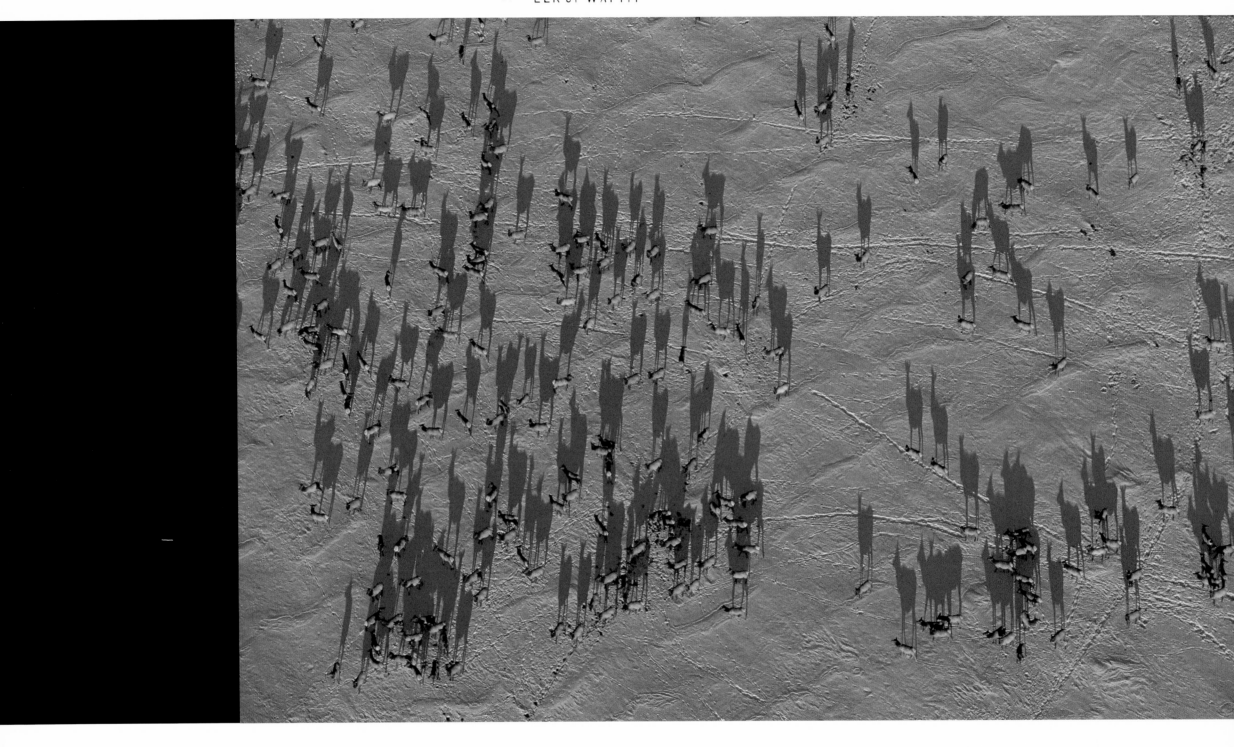

ELK or WAPITI *Cervus elaphus*

Yellowstone National Park, Wyoming

23 EMPEROR PENGUINS *Aptenodytes forsteri*

Cervus elaphus ELK or WAPITI **24**

National Elk Refuge, Wyoming

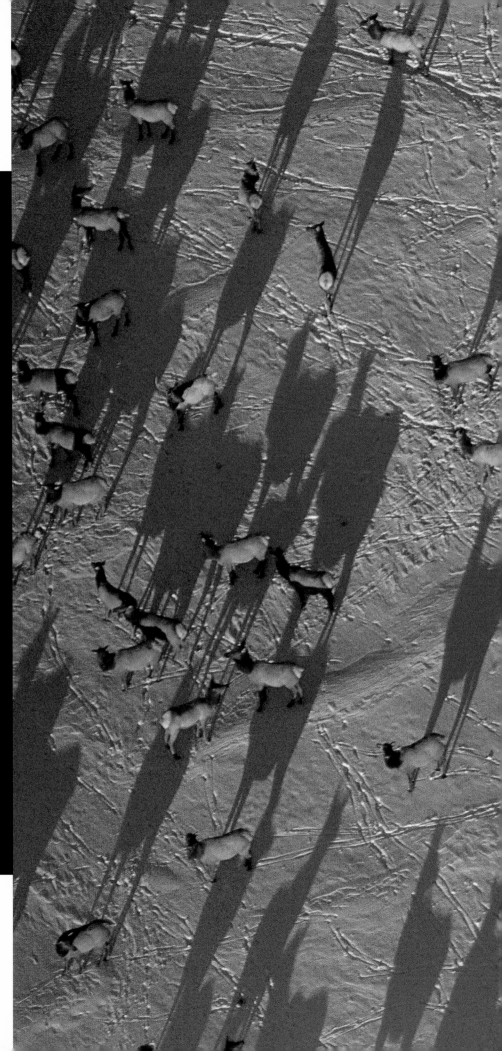

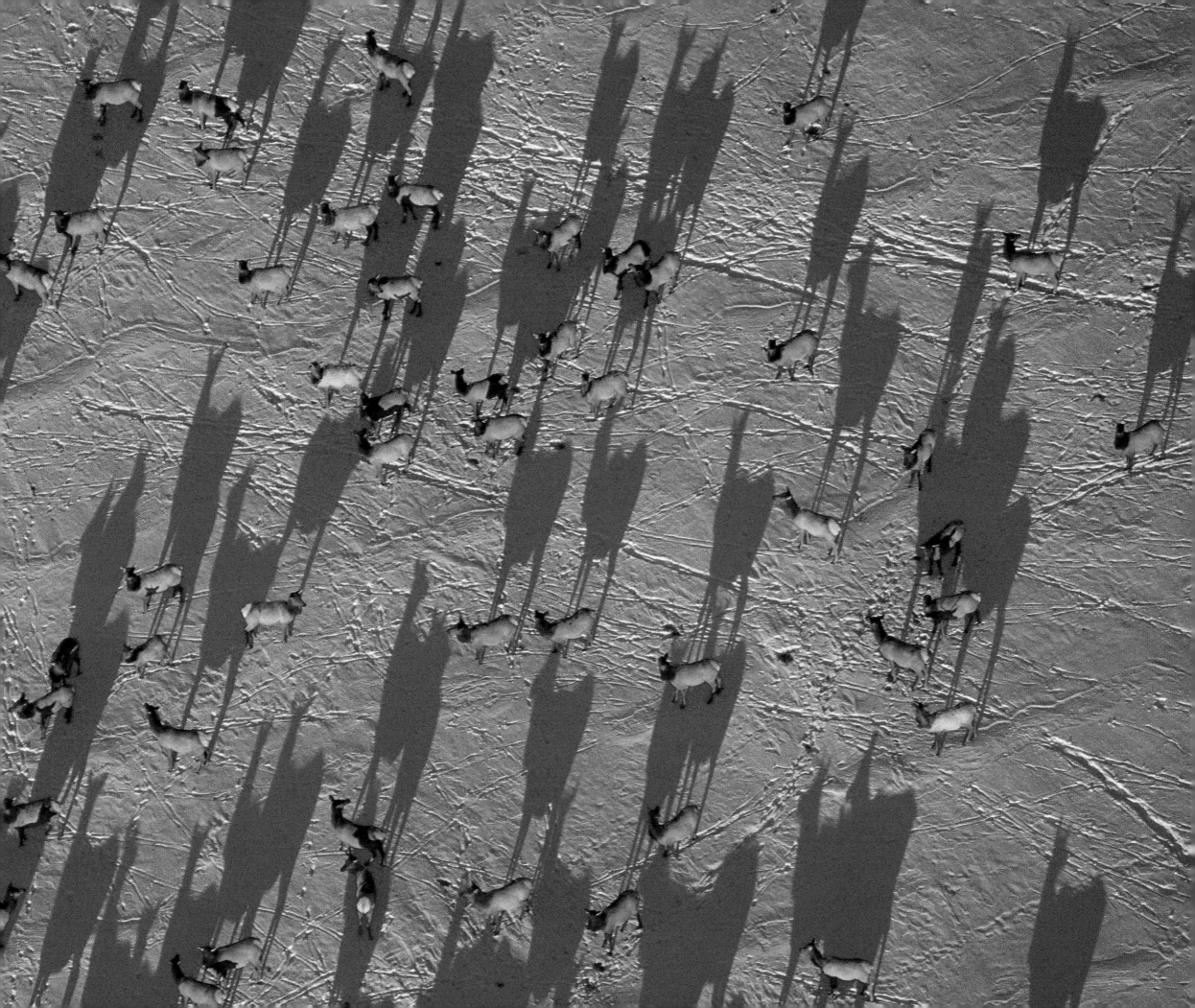

Masai Mara Game Reserve, Kenya

26   GRANT'S ZEBRAS *Equus burchelli böhmi*

Migratory mammals such as elk use traditional game trails to reach their winter range. These deeply grooved paths often persist for generations. Where rocks have been worn smooth by such passage, the trails hint at centuries of use. The Rocky Mountain Elk Foundation, based in Missoula, Montana, was established to help protect the habitat of these magnificent animals. From 1984 to 1991, the foundation raised $30 million to conserve more than one and a half million acres of critical wildlife habitat across North America. "Elk add a magical element to the land," says the foundation. "Just knowing they're out there in the hills makes you walk a little slower and look a little harder."

When the breeding season ends in the fall, male elk often face winter with fat reserves depleted after the rigorous demands of courtship. This puts them at risk for disease and starvation during the cold months ahead. Male reproductive success for an elk ultimately depends on his ability to compete with other males for access to as many breeding females as possible. Larger body size, including antler size, is directly correlated with such success—the larger the male, the more offspring he typically produces. Once the rut ends, the amount of time males invest directly in reproduction is insignificant compared to females. As the hormones subside, the males are left to feed, fatten, and grow new antlers for the next rut. In contrast, the reproductive success for a female elk depends on her ability to rear her offspring and on access to the resources necessary to make that possible. It is the female that invests the major commitment of time and energy in raising the young.

Measuring four feet tall and weighing ninety pounds, emperor penguins are the largest of all penguins. Equipped with white bellies and underparts to camouflage them from prey below, spiny fish-gripping tongues, and keen underwater vision specially adapted to the submarine hues of blue, green, and violet, penguins are superb aquatic predators. To prevent heat loss in cold water, dense fur-like feathers trap an insulating layer of warm air next to their skin.

Emperor penguins are the only bird that does not breed on land or use a nest of any kind. They breed on the Antarctic sea ice in the darkness of winter. Emperors form breeding colonies in March as the icepack begins to form. After the female lays a single egg, she leaves the male to incubate the egg nestled in fat and feathers on top of his feet, and she returns to the sea, now sixty miles distant. The male stands watch for two months, living off his fat reserves, while the female regains her strength. The thousands of males left on egg duty huddle together for warmth in Antarctic temperatures that can drop as low as minus 90 degrees Fahrenheit with winds up to 100 miles per hour. After incubating the egg without food for more than sixty days, the male then feeds the hatchling "crop milk" produced in his esophagus. The composition of this nutritive fluid has been compared to marine mammal milk both in protein content and composition. Nourished only by the male, the chick increases in weight from 300 to 600 grams. The males lose half their body weight by the time the females return to help feed the young. Until the chicks are old enough to join a crèche, both adults make fishing trips to the edge of the melting sea ice. When the ice pack breaks up in December, the emperors drift northward on a migration of ice floes.

Yellowstone is home to one of the world's largest populations of elk, estimated at more than 30,000 in the summer when the herds graze in timber basins and park meadows. In winter, some of the herds move to lower elevations outside Yellowstone, such as the National Elk Refuge at Jackson Hole, Wyoming. Three hundred years ago, an estimated 10 million elk roamed the plains of North America. Today, people are trying to save the elk that remain by establishing wilderness preserves, restricting logging and mining in prime elk habitat—and by helping to provision elk herds with food during the winter.

The gemsbok, or oryx, is a large antelope whose long straight horns are said to have given rise to the legend of the unicorn. Gemsboks are well-adapted to desert life. They walk the hot sands of the Namib Desert, where they survive long periods of drought by eating wild melons, fruits, and the bulbs of succulents. Even so, they will drink water when it is available and often walk great distances to get it. Their nomadic life-style makes it possible for them to take advantage of the vegetation bursts that follow the unpredictable desert rainfall. One day there may be a downpour, then no rain again for years. Gemsboks live in herds which vary in size depending on the availability of food and water. Their black markings, including masked faces, eye stripes, banded legs, and underlined bellies, make it difficult to tell where one gemsbok leaves off and another begins. Such dramatic coat coloration facilitates both social communication and desert camouflage.

Zebras are one of the only true wild horses left in the world today. An estimated 300,000 live on the African plains, where they often wander great distances during the dry season in search of food and water. Like all horses, these nomadic grazers are fast runners with good endurance, which enables them to outrun predators. Consequently, lions and leopards rely on ambush to capture these fleet-footed equines. Ever alert, zebras have excellent hearing, and their eyes are located high on the sides of their heads so they can keep watch while grazing. Their bedazzling stripes are thought to confuse the eyes of predators, allowing a herd of zebras to disappear in a mirage at the horizon. Because tail-gaiting and grooming are so important to the social cohesion of zebra herds, it is thought that their stripes and dramatic rump patterns may also have evolved as visual markers to direct both their following and grooming behaviors.

GRANT'S ZEBRAS *Equus burchelli böhmi*

Masai Mara Game Reserve, Kenya

28 GREAT WHITE PELICANS *Pelecanus onocrotalus*

29 GREATER SANDHILL CRANES *Grus canadensis*

30 GREATER SANDHILL CRANES *Grus canadensis*

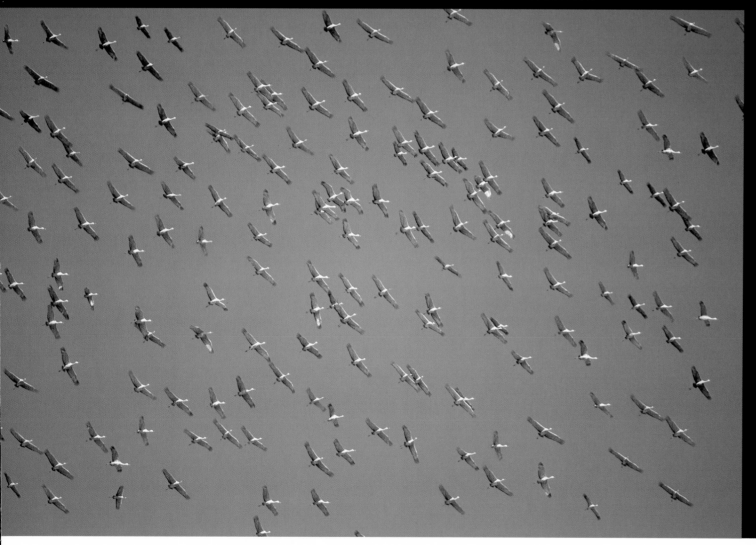

Zebras use their ears to convey mood as well as to listen for the approach of predators. Like mobile radar, their ears can swivel in all directions. When a herd of zebras stands at full attention, all eyes and ears facing forward, their body language warns that danger is near. In order to survive in the eat-or-be-eaten world of the African plains, baby zebras have to hit the ground running. Within an hour of birth, they can stand on long wobbly legs to begin their lifelong race across the grasslands.

Weighing a hefty twenty-five pounds, with short legs and oversized bills, white pelicans appear somewhat clumsy on the ground. Once airborne, their nine-foot wingspans transform them into aerodynamic sailplanes. In Africa's Rift Valley, white pelicans often fly to distant lakes in search of food, using rising hot-air currents like invisible elevators to attain the altitude needed for efficient long-distance gliding. Pelicans are notoriously social. Not only do they like to stand around together, but they like to fly together, often single file in tight formation. Skimming the waves as they ride the cushion of air between wings and water, they flap and sail in graceful unison. When they land on the water's surface, white pelicans also fish together. Grouped in semicircles, as if in a pelican aqua ballet, they dip their beaks in unison to drive fish into shallow water. When a catch is made, they throw back their heads to swallow. Their diet of fish has shaped their anatomy. The bottom half of the enormous pelican bill is covered with expandable skin. When submerged, the skin swells into a tremendous pouch used to catch fish. Pelicans also use this pouch like a shopping bag to bring home predigested food to their downy chicks. Eagerly digging deep into the pouch to gulp food, the chicks sometimes puncture their parent's skin with their sharp beaks. Pelicans do seem to hold more in their bills than they can in their bellies—about two or more pounds of fish, or roughly three gallons. During the breeding season, both the yellow-faced males and pink-faced females develop a fatty knob the size of a billiard ball on their foreheads. So adorned, they then engage in ritualized courtship behavior which includes strutting walks and group displays by males eager to impress the females. In order to nest, white pelicans need complete seclusion, such as that offered by Lake Shala in the northern part of the Rift Valley.

Flocks of greater sandhill cranes, members of the oldest living family of birds in the world, can be seen flying over the open wetlands of New Mexico's Bosque del Apache National Wildlife Refuge. The refuge is a primary wintering area for more than 12,000 of these regal birds. Six subspecies of sandhill cranes inhabit North America and Cuba. Of these, three are migratory and inhabit the West, where they winter in New Mexico, Texas, Mexico, and parts of the Gulf Coast. When they migrate, cranes fly in long lines across the sky, using rising thermals to carry them to altitudes as high as 13,000 feet. While aloft, or when alarmed, the cranes' sonorous, trumpeting calls can be heard for several miles. The calls are produced through extraordinarily long windpipes, which have been likened to French horns.

One of North America's largest birds, sandhill cranes stand up to four feet tall with a six- to seven-foot wingspan. For the most part, they are shy, wary birds. Yet John Audubon once described being driven into a river up to his neck to escape an angry sandhill crane with a broken wing. Each year, 500,000 migrating sandhill cranes converge in March along the eighty-mile stretch of the Platte River between Champman and Overton, Nebraska, to rest and refuel before continuing their migration north. With 10,000 to 20,000 birds packed per mile, it is the largest single gathering of cranes in the world, constituting roughly 80 percent of the total sandhill crane population in North America.

During the winter, as they fly between their daily feeding and roosting sites, greater sandhill cranes fill the dawn and dusk skies over Bosque del Apache. In the spring, this gregarious behavior ends when they migrate to Gray's Lake National Wildlife Refuge in Idaho and the greater Yellowstone ecosystem. The cranes pair for life and maintain their monogamous bonds by performing musical duets and elaborate bowing and leaping courtship dances at both their wintering and breeding grounds.

Following their spring migration, the crane couples stake out and defend enormous territories on which they build large mound nests. Both parents incubate the two brown-spotted eggs and attend the young. Because northern summers last only three months, young cranes must grow quickly in order to be strong enough to survive the fall migration. Sandhill cranes are especially sensitive to human disturbance and need large open areas of shallow wetlands in order to nest successfully.

Even under ideal circumstances, coyotes and ravens prey heavily on the eggs and young.

Wetlands have been called the nurseries of life because they provide a relatively sheltered, food-rich habitat for young animals, including critical breeding areas for many species of fish. Yet an estimated 200,000 acres of wetlands are destroyed in the United States every year, eliminating not only vital habitat for sedentary animals but for migratory species as well. Sandhill cranes, like all species of cranes, are well suited as symbols for wetland conservation because their very survival depends on it. The International Crane Foundation, in Baraboo, Wisconsin, is working hard to ensure that these beautiful, ancient birds survive through captive breeding programs, habitat preservation, and public education. The foundation offers a place to see not only the rare whooping cranes in captivity but all other fourteen species of cranes as well.

Chelonia mydas GREEN SEA TURTLES 31

Galapagos Islands, Ecuador

Frederick Sound, Alaska

Megaptera novaeangliae HUMPBACK WHALES 33

Green sea turtles are found throughout the warm waters of the Atlantic, Pacific, and Indian oceans. Thousands nest in the Caribbean along Costa Rica's Tortuguero beach. Those found in the Galapagos Islands and throughout much of the eastern Pacific are more brown than green in color and have a more steeply domed carapace. Between 1,200 to 3,500 female green turtles lay their eggs each year at nesting beaches located on six islands in the Galapagos. Tagging experiments have revealed that some of these turtles travel as far as the Pacific coastlines of Peru, Ecuador, Colombia, Panama, and Costa Rica before returning again to the Galapagos to lay their eggs. In other areas of the world, green turtles have been tracked swimming 2,800 miles in their circular migrations to and from nesting sites. Research conducted by the late zoologist Archie Carr showed that hatchlings enter the sea in a sort of swimming frenzy, paddling toward open sea with enough yolk attached to them to survive without food for two or three days. The frenzy subsides when the baby turtles reach huge rafts of floating seaweed, often fifty miles out to sea. They remain there to safely feed and grow until they are big enough to swim and glide around the coastal reefs and shallow-water flats.

The common honeybee is one of the most advanced species of social bees. Using a complex system of chemical communication, these nectar-feeding insects live in colonies numbering into the tens of thousands. The architectural design of their nests is as remarkable as their ability to maintain its temperature at a comfortable 34.5 to 35.5 degrees centigrade. In the winter, they warm the hive by manipulating their own body heat, forming clusters of varying size and density based on outside temperatures. Part of the brood combs are covered by these warm bee blankets. During summer, as temperatures begin to rise, adult workers cool the hive by fanning their wings. When the hive temperature exceeds 34 degrees centigrade, workers begin to carry water into the hive and attach hanging droplets over the brood cells. Others regurgitate droplets onto the tongues of their tender charges, physically extending their tongues outward to increase the rate of evaporation as workers continue to fan. Such temperature and humidity control is an adaptation found in all major groups of social insects, but one behavior sets honeybees apart from the rest, and that is their waggle dance. Performed within the nest by a returning bee, it is a ritualized re-enactment of the outward flight to a new food or nest site. The symbolic dance serves as a roadmap enabling other members of the colony to fly, unrehearsed, right to the designated spot. Honeybees are remarkable for another feat. They can fly as fast as a person can run, beating their wings 15,000 times per minute.

Weighing thirty to forty tons and reaching lengths up to forty-five feet, the singing, somersaulting humpbacks are found in all the world's oceans and adjoining seas. The humpback gets its Latin name *Megaptera*, or "big-winged," from its enormous front flippers, the largest of any cetacean. These show-stopper fins enable these gentle giants to jubilantly leap and glide through the water and to embrace their mates during amorous courtship displays. It has been said that few creatures lead a happier life or enjoy it with greater zest than the humpback. In addition to their playful acrobatics, they are the most vocal of all cetaceans, producing sirenlike serenades through their blowholes. Humpbacks produce one of the longest and most patterned songs in the animal kingdom. Heard only in the tropics during the winter breeding season, their plaintive, rhythmic moans and cries are repeated over and over for hours at a time.

Humpbacks migrate to temperate and polar latitudes to feed during summer and toward tropical latitudes to breed in winter. These bus-sized behemoths maintain their girth by eating the tiniest of prey—small fish and crustaceans. With pleated throats that expand like bellows and a mega-mouth full of stiff baleen brushes, humpbacks playfully corral their prey in a net of air bubbles.

Easily exploited by commercial whalers due to their offshore accessibility and predictable migration routes, humpbacks were nearly decimated by the middle of the twentieth century. From an original population of 125,000, as few as 3,000 remained when hunting was finally banned by international treaty in 1964. While their populations have now stabilized at around 10,000, humpbacks remain at risk. Vulnerable to pollution, increasing boat traffic, and disturbance from well-meaning whale-watchers, humpbacks also get entangled in fishing nets. More important, krill, the humpbacks' prime food resource, is now being harvested for consumption by people and livestock. Whale biologist Roger Payne has commented, "If we can't save the whales, we can't save anything." The humpback whale is another example of the international cooperation required to save an endangered species.

South Georgia Island

36   KING PENGUINS   *Aptenodytes patagonicus*

Myotis sodalis INDIANA BATS   37

Ozarks, Arkansas

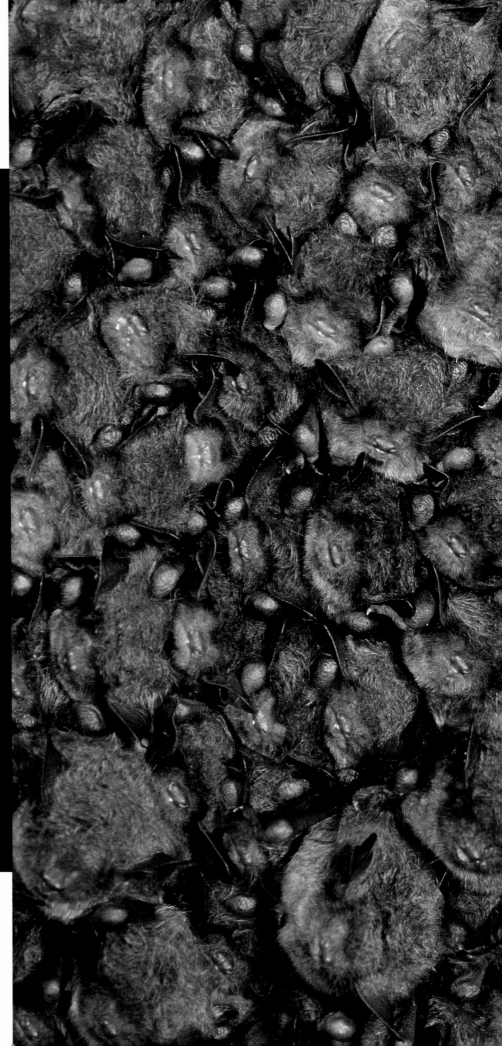

These graceful, medium-sized antelopes are easily recognized by their bold white body markings. A horizontal line delineates their two-toned rufous coat. Distinctive vertical black stripes run down their tail and rump. Impalas are highly social, living in herds of variable size. Herds of females and their young comprise the basic social unit. During the dry months, impalas join together to form larger herds whose presence is made audible by periodic grunting. When alarmed, impalas produce a high-pitched snort which warns of danger—the approach of a large feline or a pack of wild dogs.

Impalas are fleet-footed antelopes, best known for their spectacular vertical leaps made while running—even when no obstacles are present. This behavior, called *pronking*, helps them flee from predators. Active both day and night, impalas browse on acacia leaves and bushes as well as grasses and fruits. Their reproductive cycle is closely tied to the annual pattern of rainfall, with young born during the rainy season when food is most abundant. During the rut, or breeding season, males roar up to 180 times per hour, threaten and chase each other with their lyre-shaped horns, and frequently fight. These displays are an effort to win control of female herds. Impala lambs are born following a six- to seven-month gestation period. Because half are killed by predators within the first few weeks of birth, impala females have synchronized their reproduction. By giving birth at the same time, females increase the odds that their own offspring will survive by saturating predators with available prey.

Typical of all thirty species in the cormorant family, the imperial, or blue-eyed, shag is a gregarious bird. Both in coloration and bipedal stance, they are reminiscent of pelicans. Shags nest in large colonies where both parents assist in feeding their young a diet of regurgitated fish. To catch the fish, shags skillfully dive underwater using their stiff tails as rudders and their wings and pink webbed feet for propulsion. By squeezing the air out of their plumage, they lower their specific gravity, making it easier to dive and swim below the surface. However, because their feathers are not completely waterproof, cormorants must dry out their plumage after fishing. This they accomplish by basking in the sun, wings extended. To prevent overheating, the air-drying cormorants open their mouths and vibrate their throat skin, creating a highly memorable impression of a row of animated avian totem poles. Fishing underwater can be dangerous. Shags are sometimes caught and swallowed by large fish or chased and attacked by leopard seals. When they surface to swallow their catch, shags must contend with the harassment of skuas waiting to pirate their fish.

King penguins are classic colonizers. They maximize space by keeping their neighbors at beak's length, which creates an interesting visual pattern. So arranged, they use their numbers to protect themselves from the elements by forming a united front against the wind. Should the wind suddenly shift, all the birds likewise shift in order to keep the cold wind at their backs. By incubating their eggs on the top of their feet, king penguins are free to move as the weather conditions dictate, even lying prone on the ice during blizzards. Their fat and feathers envelop a single egg, creating a portable "upside-down nest" that can be transported as needed. This practical arrangement adds to the comic nature of these tuxedoed birds by creating the illusion that they have no feet at all.

King penguins can number in the tens of thousands at nesting colonies on South Georgia Island. As members of the largest family of completely flightless birds, they stand a little over three feet tall. With orange suns setting beneath their chins, matched by bright orange stripes on their bills and tear-shaped auricular patches on each side of their heads, king penguins are a sight to behold. The yellow and orange species-recognition marks concentrated around the head make it easy for penguins to identify each other while swimming. The colorful patches are also the focus of much courtship behavior such as bill- and head-rubbing between mated pairs.

Indiana bats are selective when they pick a place to hibernate. They prefer caves where temperatures average 38 to 43 degrees Fahrenheit with relative humidities of 66 to 95 percent. In these climate-controlled subterranean chambers, their metabolism slows for a long winter slumber in pitch-black darkness from October to April. Indiana bats hibernate by the thousands attached to cave ceilings, packed 300 to 480 bats per square foot. In the spring, the females warm up and depart the winter caves before the males in order to arrive at their summer maternity roosts by mid-May. The following month, females give birth to a single offspring, which they raise in maternity roosts located under loose tree bark in insect-rich woodlands bordering streams. The summer roost of adult males is often near the maternity roost. Between August and September, Indiana bats return to their hibernation caves and engage in swarming and mating activity. During this time, they build up their fat reserves for hibernation by gorging on moths and other insects until mid or late October.

Studies of Indiana bats using radio telemetry have revealed that many individuals show site fidelity—they return to the same roosting and foraging areas year after year. Indiana bats can live thirteen years or more. Huddled tightly together on a cool, damp cave ceiling, they are a poignant reminder of the fragility and persistence of life. Should they be awakened during hibernation or lose their hibernation sites, they would perish. Winter bat counts conducted between 1983 and 1989 indicated that Indiana bat populations declined by 34 percent during this period. Now listed as endangered, fewer than 400,000 of these tiny bats range over the eastern United States from Oklahoma to northwestern Florida. Because roughly 85 percent of the species hibernate at just seven cave locations, the bats are particularly vulnerable to habitat loss or disturbance during the cold winter months. Often such endangered species owe their existence to a handful of dedicated people who understand their plight and work hard to protect them. Research biologist Michael Harvey is one such individual. He not only counts the bats to record fluctuations in their numbers but helps make sure that no one disturbs them during their winter sleep.

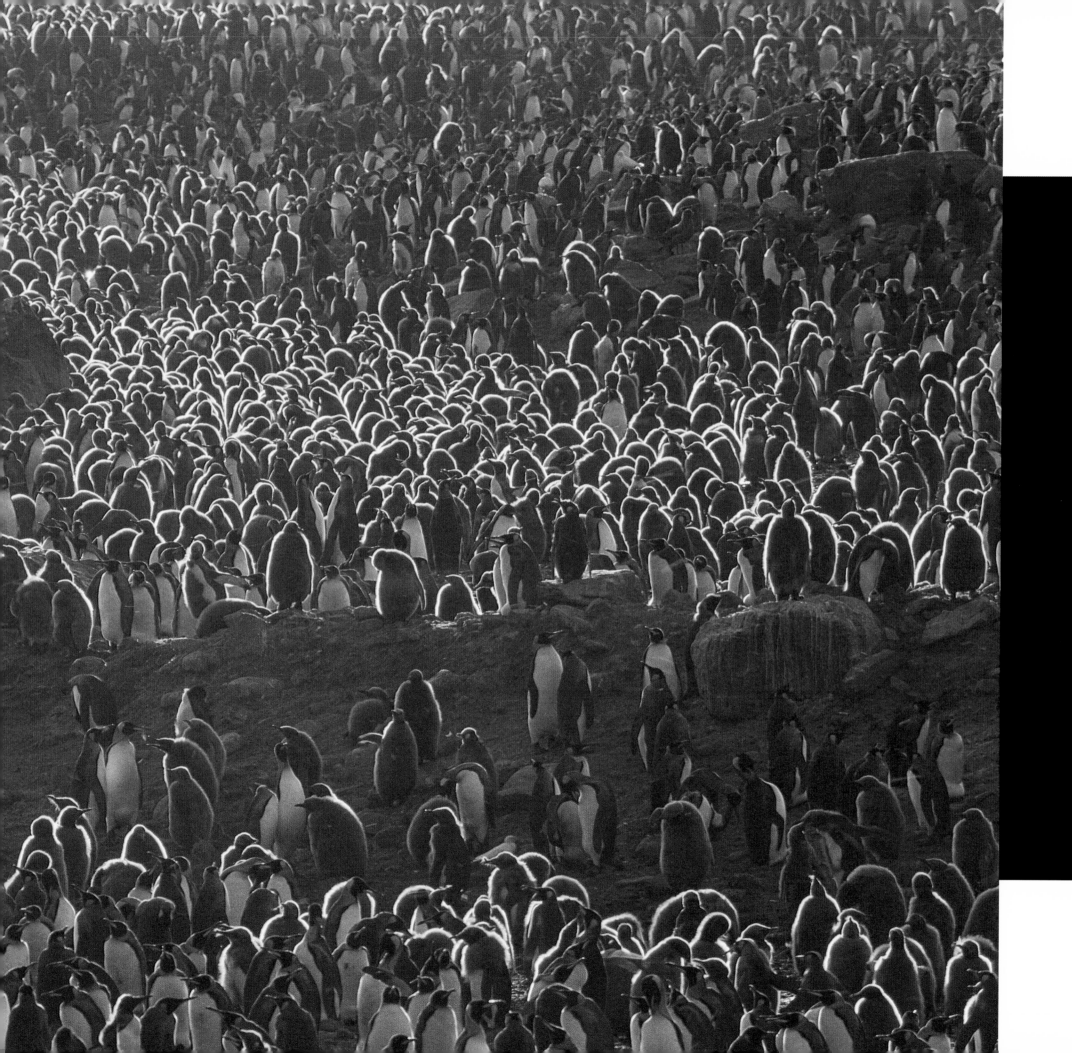

73

40 KING PENGUINS *Aptenodytes patagonicus*

South Georgia Island

South Georgia Island

41 KING PENGUINS *Aptenodytes patagonicus*

42 LADYBIRD BEETLES *Hippodamia convergens*

White Horse, Washington

Lake Magadi, Rift Valley, Kenya

43 LESSER FLAMINGOS *Phoenicopterus minor*

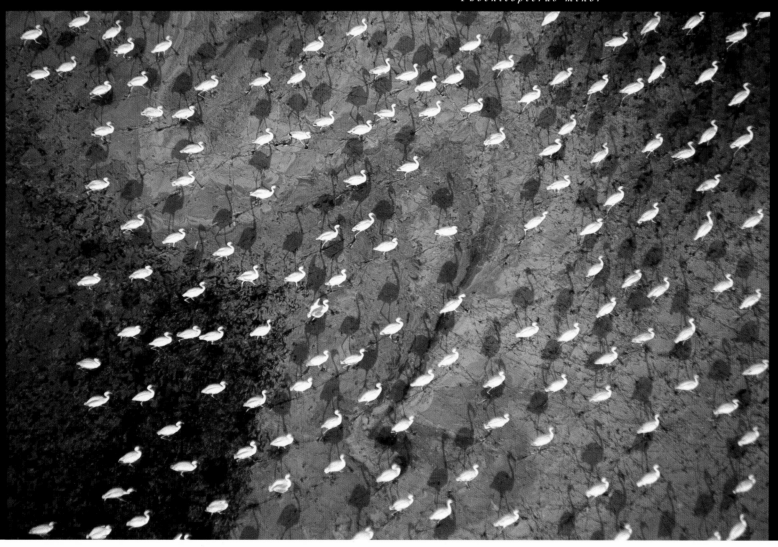

Penguins have been described as "the birds that walk like us" and as clowns in tuxedo suits that look more like animated cartoon characters than living birds. It is their many physical adaptations to life at sea that give these birds their often comical appearance—including the fact that they are nearsighted on land since their lens accommodates the refractive index of water, not air. Because penguins are relatively helpless on land, they were once routinely hunted for their pelts, eggs, and meat, and even rendered into penguin oil. Today, the threats to penguins are more insidious—commercial fishing with drift nets, ocean pollution, including tanker spills, and expanded economic development and ecotourism in the Antarctic. The penguins are also experiencing a reduction in their major food base, krill, which supports almost all Antarctic wildlife. Each year about 500,000 tons of krill are being harvested for human consumption and to produce a protein-rich chicken feed.

The king penguin is the only one of seventeen species of penguins whose young take a year or more to mature before going to sea. The king breeding cycle lasts fifteen months. A pair may breed early in the season one year, late in the season the next, and not at all in the third. This means that all king penguin chicks must pass at least one, and sometimes two, winters in a crèche. During their first winter, after being abandoned by their parents, the chicks survive entirely off their fat reserves. Still covered in baby down, they huddle together for warmth.

With seventy small feathers packed per square inch, penguins are among the most densely feathered of all living birds. The feathers overlap and are covered with a waterproofing coat of oil, giving them a sleek appearance. Early sailors—probably the same ones who believed that manatees were mermaids—thought that penguins were more closely related to fish than to birds, because their tightly overlapping feathers looked like scales. The penguin's dense coat of feathers is just one of several layers of insulation that keep the birds warm. Next comes a layer of air trapped between the feathers and the skin. Then comes the skin. And under the skin is a thick layer of fat, or blubber.

King penguin chicks are left to brave their first winter covered in fluffy brown feathers. The young penguins, appropriately called "woolies," huddle together in crèches to pass the long winter months. Feathers make up 4 to 12 percent of a bird's body weight, and so it takes energy to replace them. Mature feathers are basically dead structures that cannot grow any further. As tough as they are, feathers eventually get worn or break and require replacement. All adult birds molt at least once a year, some species as many as two or three times.

In California, the convergent ladybug hides in the forest litter of the Sierra Nevada foothills, 30 million per quarter acre. There they pass the winter months in a state of dormancy until temperatures, and their hormones, rise again. Then they mate, return to the upper valleys, lay eggs, and die. While some entomologists have expressed concern that commercial removal of these hibernating beetles may impact their overall population health, not a second thought is being given to the mass extermination of East Asian ladybugs (*Harmonia axyridis*) that recently invaded homes from Virginia to Washington. Released in the Southeast between 1978 and 1981 to kill tree aphids plaguing pecan orchards, these aggregating beetles have apparently decided that human homes are the next best thing to the granite out-croppings where they usually overwinter in Asia. Several Seattle-area homes have been invaded by 50,000 to 100,000 ladybugs crawling through the rooms and inside the walls.

Under normal circumstances, people are reluctant to kill these harmless insects. Worldwide, more than 4,000 species of ladybugs have been identified—475 in the United States alone. The name *ladybird beetle* originated from the belief that these polka-dotted insects were sent by the Virgin Mary to save crops—and since the Middle Ages, they have enjoyed a good reputation as aphid-killers. Advertised as the natural way to control pests, ladybugs can be purchased at garden stores by the pint or gallon. Pound for pound, they are voracious predators. A convergent lady-bug can eat 100 aphids in a day—its fast-crawling larvae, forty in an hour. The recent Asian ladybug infestation illustrates the potential cost of mass migration gone astray. Business has boomed for insect control at the expense of frustrated homeowners. Even benign ladybugs, it seems, given the right conditions, can become pests.

It is said that the greatest wildlife success story in East Africa's Rift Valley is that of the flamingos. More than half of the world's entire flamingo population inhabits the many salt lakes there. Just two species, the lesser and greater flamingos, contribute to this remarkable proliferation of pink-feathered birds. Of the two, the lesser flamingos are the most abundant, creating an avian ballet of long, sinuous necks and graceful, slender legs.

Phoenicopterus minor LESSER FLAMINGOS **44**

Lake Magadi, Rift Valley, Kenya

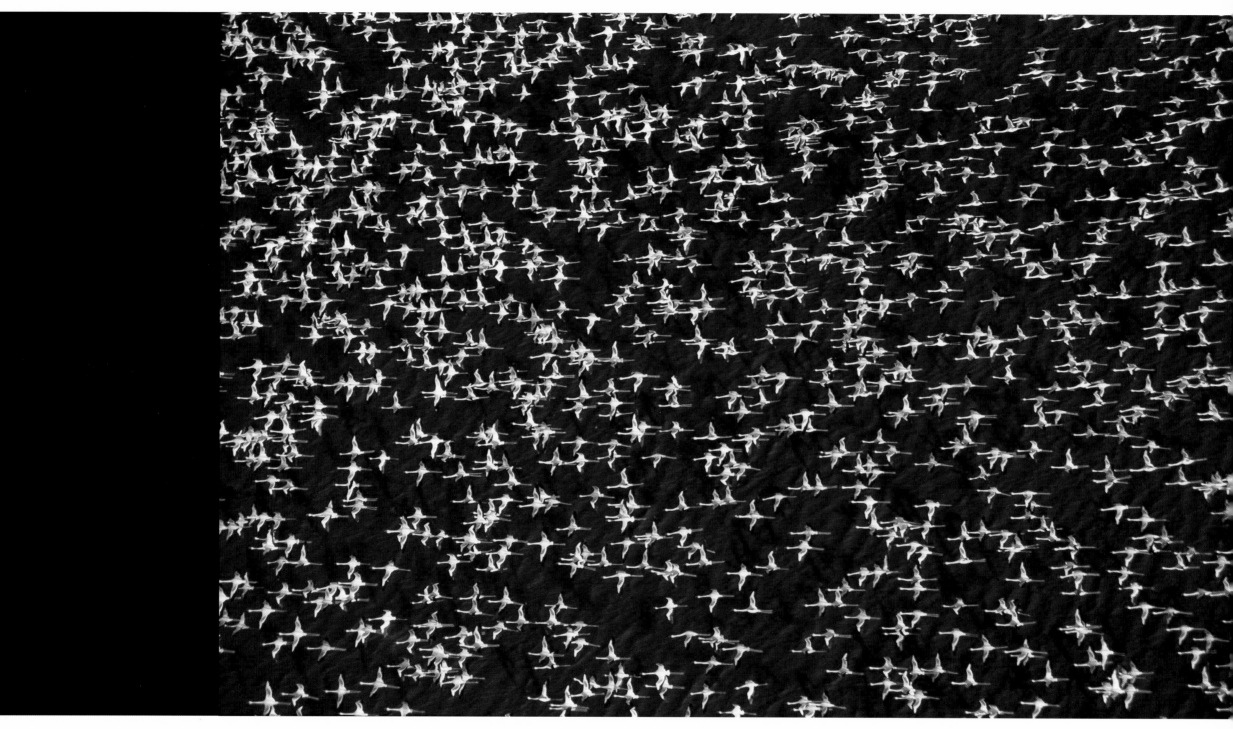

Phoenicopterus minor LESSER FLAMINGOS **45**

Lake Magadi, Rift Valley, Kenya

LESSER FLAMINGOS   **47**
Phoenicopterus minor

Lake Magadi, Rift Valley, Kenya

Lake Magadi, Rift Valley, Kenya

46   LESSER FLAMINGOS *Phoenicopterus minor*

Lake Magadi, Rift Valley, Kenya

Phoenicopterus minor LESSER FLAMINGOS **49**

Phoenicopterus minor LESSER FLAMINGOS **48**

Lake Magadi, Rift Valley, Kenya

50   LESSER FLAMINGOS *Phoenicopterus minor*

Phoenicopterus minor LESSER FLAMINGOS   51

Lake Magadi, Rift Valley, Kenya

Until the 1950s, one of the biggest unsolved ornithological mysteries was that of where the Rift Valley's three million flamingos nested. Naturalist Leslie Brown was the first to spot two large breeding colonies from the air, located several miles off-shore on the Lake Natron soda flats. His subsequent attempt to reach them on foot was nearly fatal. Setting out alone with only a small water bottle, Brown quickly discovered that the flamingos' environment was hostile, even deadly. A thin soda crust overlay a deep quagmire of sulphurous ooze, and with each step he broke through the surface to battle the foul-smelling mud. At times he crawled on his hands and knees in the hot sun, afraid to stop moving for fear of getting stuck. Fatigue finally forced him to turn back before he could reach the breeding colony. He then had to hike more than seven miles and drive another forty-five before he reached help. When Brown finally arrived in the town of Magadi, he spent three days in a hospital, and another week wrapped in bandages. While hiking, soda crystals had filled his boots and turned his legs into a minefield of painful red blisters—which turned black when exposed to air. Brown eventually tried once more to reach the isolated flamingo colony, and succeeded—but then never again set foot on the deadly shores of Lake Natron, its waters stained tomato-soup red by the algae that thrive on soda.

Flying with necks outstretched to counterbalance their long legs, flamingos are transformed into graceful aeronauts. While on the ground or while running to gain lift, however, they are vulnerable to one of their few natural predators, the Maribou stork. These heavyweight scavengers make periodic bomber runs into the pink flocks and make a meal out of any straggler, which is quickly pecked to death.

Sweeping their heads from side to side in the water, flamingos feed with their heads upside down, their club-shaped bills submerged up to their nostrils. At this angle their designer beaks, lined with transverse, toothlike ridges, are best able to strain the water for food. Using their tongues as pumps, flamingos filter water through their closed lamellate bills to retrieve particles as tiny as 1/1250 inch. While the algae they eat is nutritious, the soda broth in which it floats can be lethal. To avoid a sodium chloride overload, flamingos rely on nasal salt glands and a specialized renal system to eliminate excess salt. Because there is little competition for such a highly saline niche, lesser and greater flamingos have easily dominated the Rift.

Lake Magadi and Lake Natron lie in the deepest, hottest trough of the Central Rift Valley and are two of the most alkaline lakes in the Rift. Only sixteen inches of rain fall here each year, yet 130 inches of saline spring water and runoff evaporates from the area annually. The lakes serve as caustic heat traps where the water-soluble alkali—derived from sodium carbonate, or soda—becomes highly concentrated. The combination of heat and salt is inhospitable to most wildlife, but lesser flamingos, adapted to feed on soda algae, thrive under these harsh conditions.

A 4,000-mile fissure in the Earth's crust, the Great Rift Valley stretches from Lebanon to Mozambique. As it exits the Red Sea to travel 1,500 miles across East Africa, from Ethiopia's Danakil desert to Lake Manyara in Tanzania, the cleavage turns into a deep trench thirty miles wide marked by dramatic escarpments. This part of the Rift Valley was formed when violent underground forces tore the Earth's crust. Huge areas sunk between parallel fault lines, which forced up molten rock in a chain of volcanic eruptions. The landscape of this region continues to be a work in progress. Thirty active and semi-active volcanoes run in a string from northern Ethiopia to Tanzania. In some areas, bubbling sodium carbonate springs maintain a chain of soda lakes surrounded by blistered, lunar landscapes of crystallized salt.

Although flamingos move up and down the Rift Valley, they use Lake Magadi as their major source of food, a rich soup of algae, diatoms, and salt-tolerant aquatic invertebrates. Lesser flamingos subsist on a diet of algae, while greater flamingos augment their menu with brine shrimp and small crustaceans supported by the *spirulina* algae. This plentiful food supply attracts an estimated two million flamingos to the small four- by six-mile lake. Although the birds harvest tons of food every day, the supply is barely diminished due to the algae's fast generation in the intense ultraviolet light near the equator—and at 5,767 feet above sea level. Lake Magadi's specialized environment has created one of the greatest bird spectacles in the world.

Lesser flamingos get their red eyes and legs and rose-pink plumage from the algae they eat, which contains a pigment called carotene. This reddish hydrocarbon is present in many plants and is converted to vitamin A by the liver. Congregating in eye-dazzling flocks, flamingos use their bodies to help block the breezes that would otherwise ripple their calm feeding waters—and so gathered, they court en masse. At Lake Nakuru, thousands of birds march back and forth in a continuous, noisy parade of curled necks, raised heads, and colorful wing displays. Honking and babbling like geese, the birds eventually pair to build cone-shaped nests and produce a new generation of downy chicks.

Named after the fabled red phoenix of Greek mythology, flamingos have the longest legs in proportion to body length of any bird. There are six different species. The lesser flamingo, standing three feet tall with bright red eyes and legs, is the smallest of them all, yet they occur in such vast numbers in the East African lake district as to transform soda shorelines into an ebbing, flowing river of pink. Occasionally the vermilion-winged birds mysteriously disappear altogether in clouds of steam blown across the lakes from nearby hot springs.

Bosque del Apache National Wildlife Refuge, New Mexico
Limnodromus scolopaceus LONG-BILLED DOWITCHERS   52

George C. Reifel Migratory Bird Sanctuary, British Columbia, Canada

53 MALLARD DUCKS *Anas platyrhynchos*

55 MALLARD DUCKS *Anas platyrhynchos*

56 MALLARD DUCKS *Anas platyrhynchos* AMERICAN COOTS *Fulica americana*

George C. Reifel Migratory Bird Sanctuary
British Columbia, Canada

57 MALLARD DUCKS *Anas platyrhynchos*

This medium-sized, snipelike member of the sandpiper family frequents shallow fresh water where large flocks gather together to probe the soft mud for insects, aquatic plants, and animals. In the summer they can be found nesting as far north as Canada, Alaska, and northern Siberia. In the fall they migrate south to marshlands in the western United States and along the Atlantic coast. The name dowitcher is of Iroquois origin, and the Latin word *Limnodromus* translates as "marsh runner."

Typical of their family, they can move rapidly over the ground in search of food or to avoid trouble. Their rapid-fire probing with needle-straight bills has been likened to that of sewing machines. With their cryptic plumage, the sexes are similar in appearance, although the females are slightly larger. Both produce a single-syllable call, a simple, piercing *keek* that carries over the wetlands.

Mallards, the most abundant species of wild duck, if not the best known, are found throughout the Northern Hemisphere. From pasture ponds and park lakes to community swimming pools, mallards are a familar sight. The males' exotic colors—metallic green heads, white collars, and chestnut breasts offset by yellow bills and bright orange feet—seem commonplace. Mallards are considered the ancestor of most breeds of domestic ducks, and they have crossbred with other species of waterfowl, including black ducks and pintails. They are one of many species of "dabbling ducks," so-called for their feeding technique. Swimming with their mouths open, mallards filter food out of the water with their serrated bills. They strain gallons of water to get the food they need—basically anything that floats, including seeds, water weeds, grass, tadpoles, and fish eggs. These hardy, adaptable ducks winter as far north as water remains free of ice. Usually they arrive at their breeding grounds in the northern United States and Canada in March and April, but many nest as early as February along the warmer Pacific coast.

One of the best places to see migrating birds is at Stanley Park in downtown Vancouver, B.C., where over 230 species have been recorded. The mild winter climate and rich estuarine habitats make Vancouver and the Fraser River delta an important migratory stopover and winter destination for upwards of one and a half million birds each year. Like other species of dabbling ducks, mallards can take off in vertical flight from land or water. Such avian flight is costly. Flight generated by flapping wings, unassisted by wind or thermals, is the most metabolically expensive of all. In order to take off in still air, birds must beat their wings fast enough to overcome gravity. The lift needed to get airborne results when air is moved rapidly over the top of their wings.

In the fall, the sexes mingle as mallards form their dense winter flocks. Although they are quite tolerant of cold weather, mallards cannot remain where ice may prevent access to their main food source—aquatic plants. One safe winter haven is the 1,700-acre George C. Reifel Migratory Bird Sanctuary and adjacent Alaksen National Wildlife Area on Westham Island in the mouth of the Fraser River. This area, essential to migratory birds, has been designated a Wetland of International Significance for Waterbirds under the "Ramsar" convention. Initiated in 1971 to protect wetlands all over the globe, the convention has identified more than 350 significant wetland areas that need protection.

American coots have taken to water like ducks, yet are, in fact, members of the rail family. Their thick chalky-white bills and their habit of rhythmically pumping their heads back and forth as they swim give this fact away. Able to swim and dive with ease, these charcoal-colored birds often associate with flocks of waterfowl. While they have many different feeding strategies to obtain their mostly plant diet, one of them is to steal choice morsels from ducks.

In North America, mallard populations run in the millions. They have also been successfully introduced to Australia and New Zealand. In spring, male and female mallards express their intention to mate by swimming near each other while bobbing their heads. After mating, the female builds a nest in grass or reeds within a hundred yards of water. The ducklings hatch with their eyes open, covered with downy feathers. Within a few hours they are able to swim and dive and find their own food. Right after hatching, young ducklings single-mindedly follow the first object they see moving, which is usually their mother. This learning process, called *imprinting*, occurs during a brief critical period early in the life cycle. Should the process go awry, the results can be humorous, as Austrian behaviorist Konrad Lorenz discovered with greylag geese. Once established, the imprint is irreversible and influences all subsequent behavior patterns—especially sexual behavior.

58   MONARCH BUTTERFLIES *Danaus plexippus*

Mexico

Volga Delta, Russia

59   MUTE SWANS *Cygnus olor*

Honshu, Japan

60 NORTHERN PINTAILS *Anas acuta*

Newfoundland, Canada

Morus bassanus NORTHERN GANNETS **61**

62 NORTHERN PINTAILS *Anas acuta*

Every year, 300 million monarch butterflies from North America vanish into Mexico in what is undoubtedly the greatest of all insect migrations. They flutter from as far north as Canada and the United States east of the Rocky Mountains to twelve ancestral wintering grounds in the remote mountains of Central Mexico. There, in semidormancy, they cling together for seven months, so tightly packed on fir branches as to bejewel entire groves of trees in orange and black. The tree branches bend under the weight of 30 to 100 million butterflies packed into a three-acre area. From the air, the patch of butterfly forest glows bright orange as if on fire. The monarchs chose their winter roosting sites well. Located in Mexico's volcanic belt at altitudes over 9,000 feet, the sheltered trees sit on cool, north-facing slopes where low, moist cloud cover prevents desiccation and the tree canopy protects against winds and frost. Most important, the sites are thermally stable, with temperatures ranging from 42 to 60 degrees Fahrenheit—not cold enough to freeze the butterflies, but not warm enough to speed up their metabolism and thereby waste energy needed for flight and reproduction in the spring.

Monarchs evolved in tropical climates and are consequently unable to withstand freezing temperatures. Yet they are dependent on milkweed plants—which thrive in cooler climates—for food and protection. For this reason, monarchs spend part of the year in North America, where 100 different species of milkweeds flourish. Females lay their eggs on the underside of the toxic leaves. When the tiny caterpillars hatch three to twelve days later, they begin eating the leaves, ingesting the plants' poisonous cardiac glycosides. In just two weeks, the caterpillars grow to 3,000 times their birth weight. During the ensuing weeklong metamorphosis, the milkweed toxins are passed from caterpillar to butterfly. Birds quickly get the message to leave these brightly colored insects alone, as the bad-tasting toxins make them vomit.

With their food source in the temperate zone and their winter roosting areas in the tropics, monarchs solved the distance problem by becoming the only species in their family that migrates. Weighing one-fifth of an ounce, the fragile insects can fly eighty miles in a day. They reach their summer destinations by leapfrogging north in successive generations—several generations are born, breed, and die before the last generation reaches Canada in time for the winter migration south. With no previous knowledge of the route or the destination, the last generation fuels up on flower nectar and then flies by instinct 2,000 miles south to Mexico—right back to the same three-acre patch of forest. Propelled on breezes at speeds up to thirty-five miles per hour, these "flying flowers" make the return trip in six weeks.

Unlike the native whistling and trumpeter swans, which swim with their necks erect and bills level, mute swans swim with graceful curves to their necks, bills pointing downward. These beautiful, well-known water birds are social except when breeding, at which time pairs break away from the flock to build large isolated nests of plant material in which the female lays five to eight white eggs. Parents often let their hatchlings ride on their backs for warmth and protection from predators. The soft calls produced during the breeding season change to threatening grunts and hisses as the swans defend their nests and young. At other times they are as quiet as their name suggests. The mute swan was imported to America from Eurasia sometime during the middle of the nineteenth century to add beauty to parks and estates. The swans flourished and spread into the countryside. Today, thousands live wild along the mid-Atlantic coast and around the Great Lakes. Big and domineering, these thirty-pound birds illustrate one of the problems associated with feral species. Mute swans can be as belligerent as they are beautiful, easily driving native waterfowl from their nesting and feeding areas. Once imported, feral species can run amok, their original function lost to a host of unanticipated problems.

With the rapid wing beats typical of most ducks, pintails are fast, graceful fliers. During takeoff, they leap out of the water and launch immediately into the air. As with other dabbling ducks, pintails feed almost exclusively in shallow water on a diet that includes everything from seeds and plants to crayfish, worms, and aquatic insects. Pintails search for food by bobbing at the surface, "tails up," and extending their long necks underwater. They maintain this feeding position with forward thrust from their paddling webbed feet.

The northern gannet is the only member of the booby family that nests in northern latitudes. They winter along the eastern coast of the United States from Massachusetts south to Florida. At their summer rookeries farther north, they utilize every available niche to build their nests. Quarreling over space is common. When hungry, gannets turn into fish-seeking missiles, plunging into the water from heights of fifty feet or more. A reinforced skull and air cells in their chest and neck help to absorb the impact. Hatchlings are fed a diet of partially digested fish regurgitated by both parents. The adults take turns guarding their nest, using a series of vocalizations and displays that help the approaching mate find its nest and partner among thousands. The start of the southward migration in September is a tough time for young gannets. Too fat to fly, they jump or fall off cliffs and glide into the sea. Learning how to fish and waiting until their wings are strong enough for sustained flight, they survive for several weeks on their body fat. Under fledgling conditions such as these, it is little wonder that only 26 percent of young gannets survive their first year, and only 18 percent reach adulthood. One of the largest northern gannet rookeries in North America is located on Bonaventure Island in the Gulf of St. Lawrence. Approximately 45,000 birds congregate there every summer.

Found in ponds and lakes throughout the Northern Hemisphere, these familiar dabbling ducks are second only to the mallard in abundance. Their nickname, "sea pheasants," refers both to their coloration and palatability. Pintail females resemble female mallards in their cryptic brown plumage, but they have longer necks and pointed tails. A coating of oil on their feathers keeps them waterproof and warm, even in the coldest weather.

Pintails begin their northern migration to spring nesting sites early in the new year. Females build nests of moss, leaves, sticks, and grass, lining them with their own downy feathers. Feathers are important to all waterfowl, making it possible to fly, stay waterproof and warm, and advertise the identity of their species to others. A single duck may be covered with more than 11,000 feathers. These it carefully preens, literally zipping up the barbules, or spines, of each feather to keep them structurally waterproof. While preening, ducks also coat their feathers and the scales of their feet with an oily substance produced by a special heart-shaped gland located above the base of the tail. This secretion of fatty acids, wax, and fat helps waterproof the feathers and maintain the gloss and surface structure of the bill. It is also said to contain a precursor of vitamin D, which when activated by sunlight, may help prevent the development of rickets in some birds.

64 PACIFIC DOUBLE-SADDLE BUTTERFLYFISH *Chaetodon ulietensis*

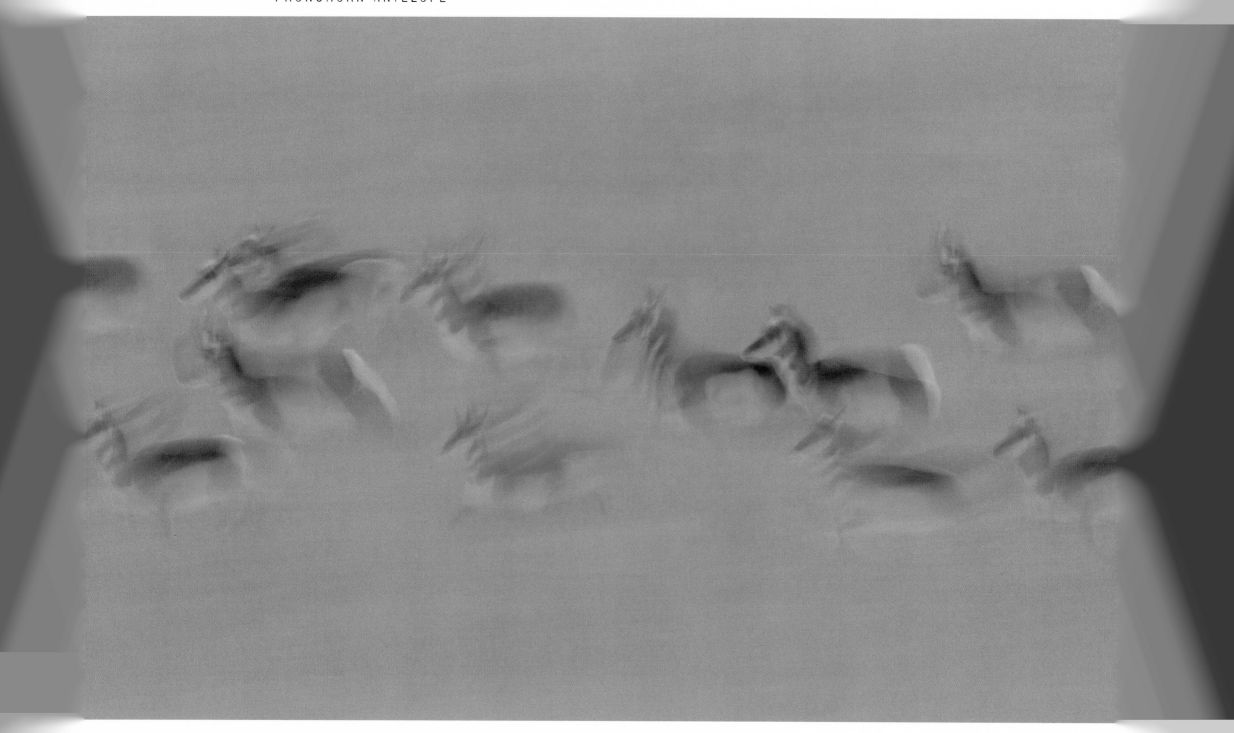

Okavango Delta, Botswana

Quelea quelea RED-BILLED QUELEA **66**

112

Hokkaido, Japan

67 RED-CROWNED CRANES *Grus japonensis*

68   RED-WINGED BLACKBIRDS *Agelaius phoeniceus*

Butterflyfish are day-active predators that feed on benthic invertebrates. They use vision to find their prey and feed on conspicuous reef invertebrates such as sponges, tunicates, corals, and mollusks. To avoid being eaten, these prey species have gone to great extremes, developing spines, heavy armor, toxins, and even inpalatable tastes in order to thwart attack. In what amounts to an evolutionary arms race between predator and prey, fish such as the butterflyfish have had to become increasingly specialized in order to overcome these invertebrate defenses. Some butterflyfish, armed with small sharp teeth, sneak up on armored prey to snip off pieces of their soft parts that are exposed when they feed. Others dine on the tentacles of polychaete worms and the mucus secreted by corals.

Butterflyfish have developed a few tricks of their own in order to avoid being eaten. Their stout dorsal and anal spines make them tough to swallow, and in a pinch, they can swim backwards. With pancake-thin bodies, they can wedge themselves into inaccessible cracks. Their bright colors and pattern of vertical black stripes help to break up the outline of their bodies. The black lines also cause a camouflage effect called "flicker fusion" to occur in the eyes of predators. When a striped fish swims across a field of vertical plant stems, the rapid movement of the stripes across the stems causes them to fuse, creating an optical illusion that makes the fish disappear.

Pronghorns are not true antelope at all, but even-toed ungulates that belong to the bovid family. They are named for their two-pronged horns, which the males shed at the end of their breeding season. Their beautiful tan and white markings, unusual for North American ungulates, are used to communicate across the open grasslands. To warn of danger, they can raise the white hairs on their rump to produce a flash of white that can be seen for two miles or more. Pronghorns are known for speed, endurance, and distance, and they can average forty-five miles per hour over four miles. Prior to the late 1800s, 40 to 50 million pronghorns grazed the open plains of North America, seasonally migrating in search of the most available food. Although

these high-speed mammals have been clocked running as fast as fifty-five miles per hour, they couldn't run faster than a speeding bullet, and by 1920 only 13,000 survived. In addition to hunting and habitat loss, part of their decline can be blamed on their incurable curiosity. Pronghorns will approach anything that moves, from predators to a handkerchief waved at the end of a pole. The latter, called "flagging," was a technique used by hunters to bring the antelope within gunshot. This practice, now illegal, contributed to the rapid decline of these big-eyed bovids. Today, more than 450,000 pronghorns exist, the result of effective management and conservation measures.

Like a swarm of locusts, enormous flocks of red-billed quelea can block the sun in densities so great as to make flocks of European starlings look paltry. Occurring in noisy, chattering flocks of hundreds, thousands, even millions of birds, red-billed quelea have replaced locusts as the primary threat to African seed-growing farmers.

From a distance, the flocks look like fast-moving clouds of smoke. Should such an avian cloud of quelea descend on a farmer's crops, his harvest is as good as gone due to the speed with which these tiny birds can devour seeds and demolish vegetation. Related to weavers, quelea nest in large colonies in thorn trees and reed-beds.

Before roosting for the night, they usually swarm at a river or waterhole to drink—often while in flight. Because of their sheer numbers, some may be pushed into the water and drown, and others may be snapped up by crocodiles. When they finally settle down for the night, the tiny birds cover every available inch on trees and bushes, their combined weight often breaking the branches on which they roost.

Long a favorite subject of Asian paintings and legends, the rare red-crowned crane, sometimes called the Japanese or Manchurian crane, is one of the most beautiful of the world's fifteen species of cranes. Native to Japan, Korea, China, and Russia, this large bird stands an impressive four feet tall. Its snow-white feathers are offset by designer-black legs, head and neck stripes, and a large pompadour of black tertial feathers.

Cranes are graceful wading birds that inhabit open wetland marshes and plains. There they feed on grains, fleshy plant roots, and a variety of small animals. Leaping high into the air with wings half open, courting pairs run around each other in circles, bow, and then leap some more in joyful "dances." Their long coiled windpipes enable them to produce loud, long-distance trumpeting calls during the breeding season and migration.

In contrast to their winter densities, each mated pair requires an enormous area of marshland in order to breed in the spring. Both males and females defend their territory, build a ground nest, and tend the eggs and young. Like other crane species, the red-crowned crane is restricted to relatively small breeding areas—one of the main reasons it is now endangered. Another contributing factor is the cranes' incredible site fidelity. They continue to return to their traditional breeding grounds, even after the habitat has been destroyed.

Nearly extinct at the turn of the century due to hunting and wetland drainage, the red-crowned crane survives today in two separate populations. One breeds in southeastern Siberia and China, migrating to Korea in winter. The Japanese population is sedentary, breeding only on the island of Hokkaido. Dairy farming, forestry, heavy industry, and highway development continue to threaten the Japanese population, along with mortality from power-line collisions.

In 1935, the Society for the Preservation of the Japanese Crane was formed in Japan, the same year that the species was designated a Natural Monument. South Korea designated the red-crowned crane as Natural Monument No. 202 in 1968. Ironically, this highly endangered species is considered the symbol for longevity in Japan. Ultimately, the species' own longevity will depend on the strict protection of its remaining marshlands.

During the breeding season, male red-winged blackbirds cling to cattail stalks and perch high atop bushes to flash their bright red shoulder patches. This visual display warns rival males to keep their distance, while at the same time advertising the male and his territory to passing females. Sparring, displaying male blackbirds sometimes perch side by side, their bills pointing skyward. The contest changes with the onset of autumn. In order to survive to breed again, male territoriality is suppressed, enabling the birds to gather peacefully in enormous flocks at the limited winter refuges offering adequate food and water.

71 SCARLET IBIS *Eudocimus ruber*

Caroni Swamp, Trinidad

72 SCARLET IBIS *Eudocimus ruber* CATTLE EGRETS *Bubulcus ibis*

Red-winged blackbirds, known for their gurgling spring songs, are thought to be the most numerous land birds in North America. Numbering in the thousands, huge winter flocks swarm to feed on weed seeds and waste grain. Red-winged blackbirds are just one of 320 species of birds that attract 100,000 people each year to New Mexico's Bosque del Apache National Wildlife Refuge. Although the area was established by the U.S. Fish and Wildlife Service in 1939 as a wintering refuge, primarily for geese, ducks, and sandhill cranes, it also serves as home to a tantalizing array of other species, from shorebirds and waders to songbirds and raptors. The refuge is one of 500 national refuges, encompassing nearly 90 million acres, that is managed by the U.S. Fish and Wildlife Service.

There are twenty-one species of crocodilians in the world, all virtual relics from prehistoric times. They evolved more than 200 million years ago and have inhabited tropical swamps and estuaries since dinosaurs dominated the planet. Fossil evidence shows that primitive alligators existed in both Montana and China at least 70 million years ago. With changing climates and continental shifts, species have come and gone. An extinct species of Madagascar crocodile once reached lengths of thirty feet or more.

All crocodilians are specially designed for an aquatic life of swimming and drifting. With nostrils that lie on the raised tip of their nose, and eyes and ears located high on their head, they can breathe, see, and hear while nearly submerged. Their tough hide is formed of hundreds of rectangular scales. Bony plates embedded in the scales give them their armored look. Their coloration provides perfect camouflage in murky water.

Like all reptiles, crocodiles are cold-blooded and must regulate their body temperature by balancing combinations of heat and cold in their environment. It might appear that their preferred activity is dozing in the sun, but this behavior results from their need for warmth when water temperatures are cool. Because a crocodile's heavy skull heats up faster than the rest of its body, it opens its enormous mouth to let evaporation help keep its head from overheating. Crocodiles need heat from the sun to activate digestive enzymes. Lack of sunshine can kill a crocodile with a full stomach because the food will rot instead of being digested. Without a shot of energizing sunshine, sluggish crocodiles can even drown in cold water.

Crocodiles are formidable predators. More than 70 percent of their body weight is skin and muscle. Armed with sharp teeth and powerful tails, crocodiles catch their prey through ambush, leaping out of the water to grab a leg or snout. Huge muscles snap their jaws shut with tremendous force, making it difficult for prey to escape. Once caught, prey is dragged into deeper water, and the crocodile rolls underwater with the prey until it drowns. Lacking molars, crocodiles can't crush or grind fresh food. Instead, they shake and slap the carcass against the ground or water surface to rip off bite-sized pieces. To aid this process, crocodiles often store their food in an underwater den or drag it around in their mouths for several days until it rots enough to be eaten. Saltwater crocodiles are the largest living reptiles in the world. Some measure more than twenty feet in length. Crocodiles have large brains for a reptile, making them one of the smartest.

With their heads thrust forward and long legs trailing, these flame-red birds alternately flap and soar in synchrony. In the late-afternoon glow of sunset, they set their roosting trees ablaze with color. Ibis belong to an ancient group of birds whose fossil record dates back to the Eocene, sixty million years ago. As recently as 5,000 years ago, the sacred ibis was worshiped by the Egyptians, who included them in their religious beliefs and written records, and mummified them for burial with the pharaohs. While the sacred ibis has not bred in Egypt for more than a century, the scarlet ibis is protected as the national bird of Trinidad. Native to the tropical mangrove swamps, muddy estuaries, and tidal flats along the coasts and beaches of northern South America, these gregarious birds roost in large numbers. Even their nestlings socialize early, climbing about in the trees two to three weeks before they are able to fly. Both sexes look alike. Their long, downcurved bills are used to probe the mud for crabs and mollusks. All species of ibis native to North America are currently protected by law.

Scarlet ibis are stunning birds. Not only is their flame-red color remarkable, but there is a sacred quality to their profile, a hint of the ancient past. These long-legged wading birds forage primarily by touch, using their long curved bills to probe the shallow water and soft mud until they make contact with prey. During courtship the male and female intertwine their slender bills and necks in a ritualized dance. Aggressive displays occur when males compete for the attention of a female. During such encounters, they fly up, face each other, and fence with their long bills. The salt marshes where ibis are found provide them with insects and crustaceans for food.

Unlike most species of herons and egrets, cattle egrets hunt almost exclusively on land, often in close proximity to grazing mammals that help stir up insects. Little wonder that egrets have been observed threatening each other in defense of these traveling feeding sites. It has been estimated that by associating with cattle, foraging egrets increase their prey capture rate by 50 percent while expending only two-thirds the energy needed to hunt alone. This symbiotic relationship benefits both bird and host. The mammals flush out insects for the birds to eat, and the birds de-tick the mammals and help reduce the herbivorous insects that compete with the mammals for food. Tractors are an acceptable substitute if no livestock is available. Dozens of egrets have been observed following behind a plow. Although grasshoppers are their preferred fare, cattle egrets are opportunistic feeders, also eating frogs, snakes, beetles, and small nesting birds. To help control flies, cattle egrets were introduced to the Seychelles, the Hawaiian Islands, and the Chagos Archipelago. Because they also like to gulp seabird chicks, their presence on these islands has been a mixed blessing.

During courtship, the adult develops striking orange-buff highlights around the crown, nape, lower neck and back, and the legs turn scarlet. Breeding colonies consist of hundreds, even thousands of pairs of egrets. Cattle egrets, like all members of the heron family, are capable of sustained long-distance flight. Seasonal migrations and extensive post-breeding dispersals are typical of the group. Cattle egrets regularly fly to remote islands in the Atlantic as much as 1,700 miles from the African mainland.

73 SNOW GEESE *Anser caerulescens*

Bosque del Apache National Wildlife Refuge, New Mexico

74   SNOW GEESE *Anser caerulescens*

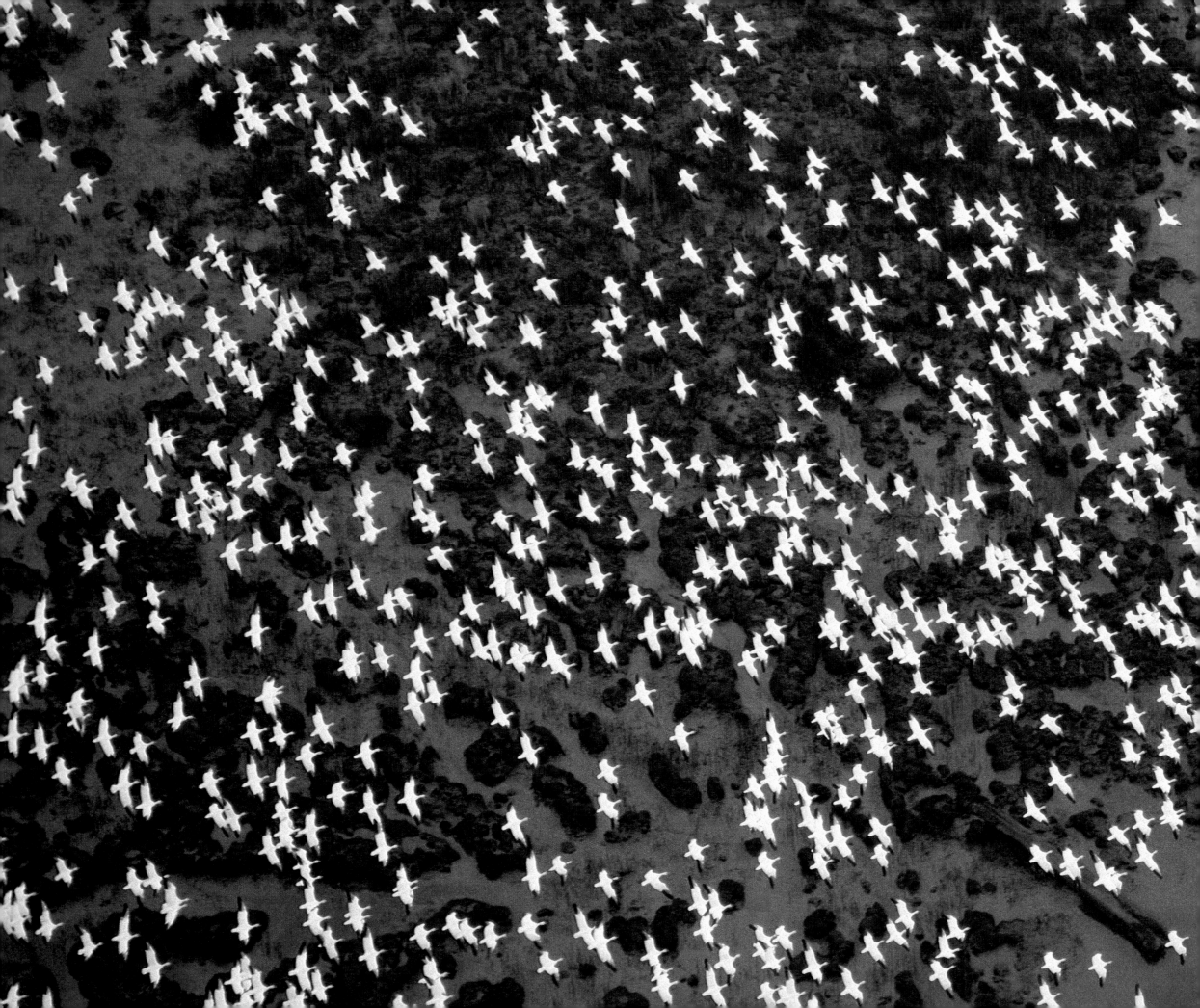

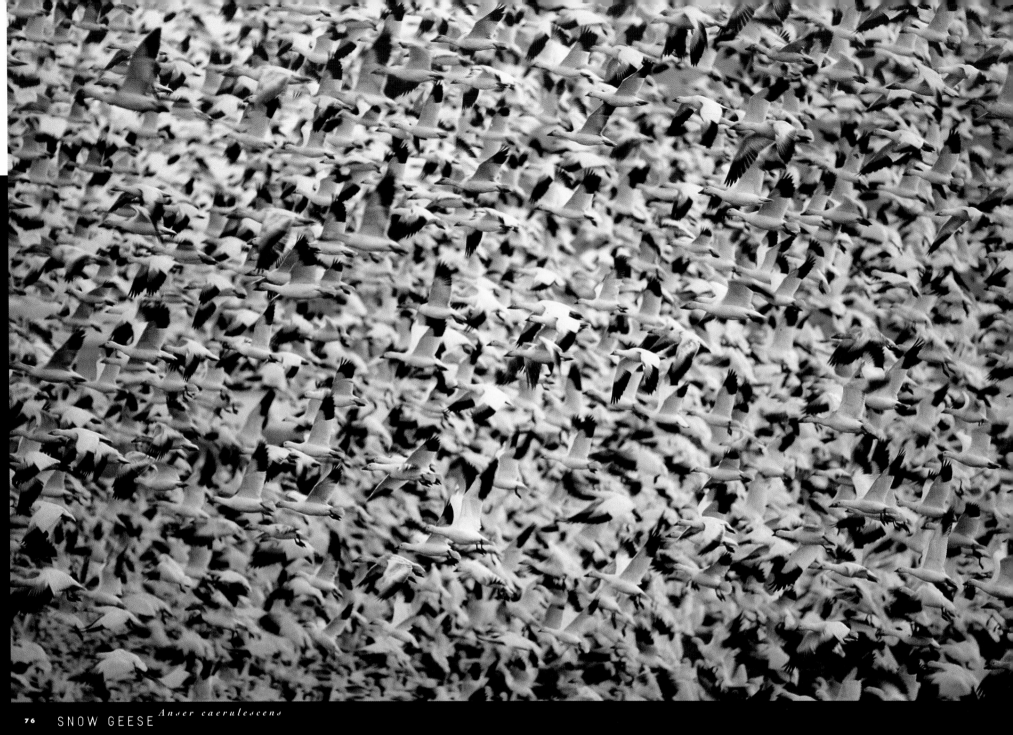

76 SNOW GEESE *Anser caerulescens*

Tule Lake, California

Anser caerulescens SNOW GEESE **77**

Bosque del Apache National Wildlife Refuge
New Mexico

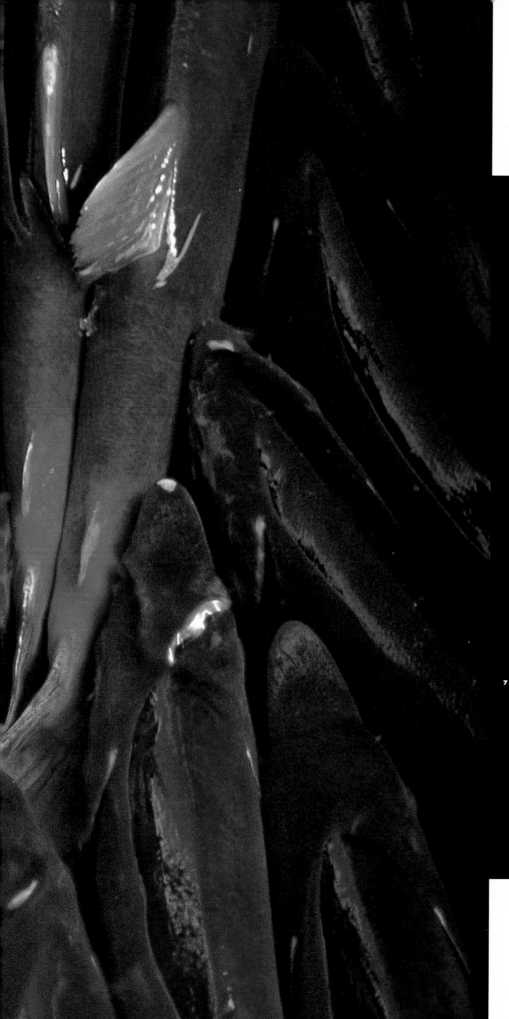

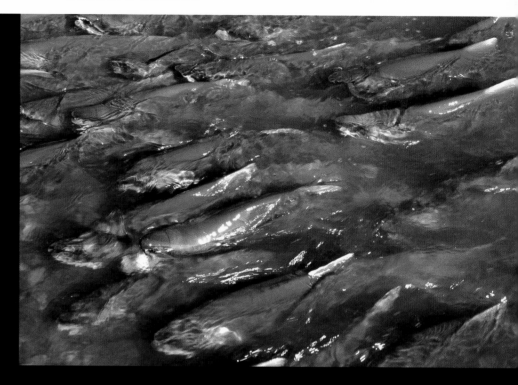

79 SOCKEYE SALMON *Oncorbynchus nerka*

78 SOCKEYE SALMON *Oncorbynchus nerka*

Wood River Lakes region, Hansen Creek, Alaska

Nearly 60,000 snow geese winter in the middle Rio Grande Valley each year, making Bosque del Apache National Wildlife Refuge the most popular birding site in New Mexico. Snow geese occur in both a white and a blue phase. The black pigment at the tips of their wings is thought to make their flight feathers more resistant to wear. These long feathers, called *primary feathers*, can be spread out like the fingers of a hand to manipulate the air in flight. The feathers of albino snow geese, lacking such pigment, are more brittle, which probably affects their ability to fly. Like airplanes, a bird's rate of energy consumption is most efficient when pushed by tail winds at high speed and altitude.

There are definite advantages to flying in formation. As each bird flies, some air is lost over the wing tips, causing the bird a loss in lift. By flying in V-formation, snow geese take advantage of the spiraling wingtip vortices and upwelling air created behind the wings of the leading birds. Each flying bird creates a small area of disturbed air behind it called a slipstream. If birds flew directly behind each other, they would be caught in this turbulence and thrown off course. By flying slightly beside or above each other, a second bird can literally rest its inner wingtip on the rising vortex of air produced by the lead bird to receive energy-saving lift. As a result, older and stronger birds usually take the lead with the younger and weaker birds positioned farther back in the slipstream where the flying is easier. It is estimated that by migrating in V-formation, birds can fly as much as 71 percent farther than they could if alone.

The word *fat* seems a contradiction in terms when considering avian adaptations for flight—such as hollow bones, thin skulls, and lightweight feathers. Yet body fat provides both energy and insulation, and it fuels long-distance migration. It also allows birds to shiver as a means of generating body heat to keep warm. Fat is an extremely efficient fuel because it is so energy-dense. Each gram of fat yields roughly twice the energy produced by a gram of protein or sugar. Just as jets are topped off before a transoceanic flight, birds fuel up on high-fat foods before long-distance migrations. Studies have shown that the most dominant birds carry the heaviest reserves of fat. Their dominance not only gives them better access to fat-producing foods but to the warmest, safest positions deep within flocks and roosts. The least dominant birds are pushed to the periphery of the flock, where they more easily succumb to bad weather and predation.

SNOW GEESE *Anser caerulescens* .... Tule Lake, California

After Canada geese, snow geese are the second most abundant of all the world's wild geese. Each fall, the need for food, water, and warmer temperatures forces many species, like the snow geese, to cast their fates to the wind and brave the dangers of migration. In the process, weather and distance cull the weakest, leaving only the strongest to breed in the spring. Drawn to the millions of waterfowl that gather at winter refuges each fall, bald eagles capitalize on this selection mechanism. Healthy geese are too active for an eagle to kill, so in much the same manner that they feed on dead and dying salmon, the eagles attack only the sick or injured birds that are already stranded on the ground.

77 SNOW GEESE *Anser caerulescens* .... Bosque del Apache National Wildlife Refuge, New Mexico

Radar studies indicate that more birds migrate at night than by day, generally traveling with the wind at high elevations. By aiming a telescope at the full moon, or "moon-watching," it is possible to get a glimpse of these nocturnal travelers. The heaviest traffic seems to occur from shortly after dark until midnight. One advantage of flying undercover at night is that the birds are then free to rest and forage by day. During fall and winter, migrating flocks of snow geese find nourishment in the underground rhizomes of marsh plants.

78 SOCKEYE SALMON *Oncorhynchus nerka* .... Wood River Lakes region, Hansen Creek, Alaska

After migrating thousands of miles in the open ocean, sockeye salmon return to spawn within yards of their birthplace. Salmon partially use topographical features to navigate, but they rely primarily on olfaction to relocate their freshwater birth streams. Fish have a keen sense of smell, and each river has its own odor signature created by the vegetation and soil. In addition, each genetic stock of salmon produces its own unique odor tag by releasing pheromones into the water. During the return migration, males sport vivid spawning colors and develop pronounced hooks and large canine teeth—and both sexes stop feeding. The journey upstream is difficult, and many never reach their spawning grounds. Those that do will die, exhausted, shortly after mating. Females lay two to four thousand eggs in gravel nests, or redds, which they guard until they die. The eggs hatch following a sixty-day incubation period. Sockeye fry live in large lakes for twelve to twenty-four months before they migrate downriver to the sea.

79 SOCKEYE SALMON *Oncorhynchus nerka* .... Wood River Lakes region, Hansen Creek, Alaska

Many species of pelagic fish make regular seasonal movements and migrate long distances. Salmon are unique in that they spend time in fresh water at both the beginning and the end of a life cycle that also takes them out to sea. While at sea, the maturing salmon feed on baitfish and zooplankton, which thrive only in a narrow range of ocean temperature and salinity. Should surface temperatures rise more than a few degrees above normal, the production of zooplankton may be reduced, causing salmon populations to decline. Salmon are equally sensitive to changing river conditions. Because the ecological balance they require is so precise, salmon are a good indicator of the overall health of an environment. Their loss serves as a quiet warning.

Okavango Delta, Botswana

81 SOUTHERN CARMINE BEE-EATERS *Merops nubicoides*

82 SOUTHERN ELEPHANT SEALS *Mirounga leonina*

South Georgia Island

Round Island, Alaska

Odobenus rosmarus WALRUS 83

Salmon are to the Pacific Northwest what bison were to the Midwest. They are intricately woven into the culture, history, and spirituality of the region. The annual return of the fighting, leaping fish has traditionally brought a renewal of life, not just for the spawning salmon, but to the many people and animals that depend on them as a source of food. In 1992, "Lonesome Larry" was the only sockeye salmon to return to Idaho's upper Salmon River. His precious sperm was frozen and used to fertilize one of the only two sockeye females that returned to Idaho in 1993.

Conservation efforts to restore salmon runs in the Columbia River system now cost more than $300 million a year in taxes and lost power revenues. In 1994, virtually all commercial and recreational salmon fishing was banned along the Pacific coast from Mexico to Canada as a last-ditch effort to protect salmon stocks near extinction due to loss of habitat, overfishing, and warm ocean waters. The Clinton administration subsequently agreed to pay $16 million in federal disaster relief to the Northwest coastal communities hardest hit by this historic ban.

The fluttering movement and brilliant darting colors of a carmine bee-eater colony are a feast for the eyes. Both sexes are equally colorful—bright red with turquoise highlights. One could easily spend hours watching the social antics and skillful feeding aerobatics of these avian fireballs as they energetically go about their day. As their name implies, they do subsist on bees, but they will also eat other insects, which they adroitly capture on the wing—either while soaring or by darting from stationary perches. These high-speed little birds even utilize brushfires as part of

their feeding strategies by foraging along their insect-flushing edges. Bee-eaters nest and roost in large colonies. Like riverbank condominiums, their sandbank burrows are constructed in close proximity. During the breeding season, devoted parents feed their young nonvenomous insects while they are in the nest, then teach them the dangerous art of devouring bees, their primary prey, once they can fly. Carmine bee-eaters breed in southern Africa from September to March, and then migrate to the tropics in April.

The southern elephant seals of the subantarctic are the largest of all seals. More than 300,000, nearly half the world population, are based on South Georgia Island. The seals get their name from the "trunks," up to eleven inches long, that dangle off the end of the males' noses. During conflicts, these protuberances are inflated like balloons to exaggerate the size of the males' massive heads and help resonate their threatening snorts and roars. Elephant seals gain their girth by eating large fish and squid, often caught at great depths. Mature bulls are considerably larger than females, showing the most extreme sexual dimorphism among the true seals. During the breeding season, beachmasters clumsily patrol their territories, ready to do battle. Should a challenger not back down, the two embattled males rear up to bash each other with their heads and bodies until one tires and retreats.

For the most part, southern elephant seals coexist peacefully with penguins on the island shores. However, their enormous size makes the penguins look like a gathering of sand fleas. Occasionally, the seals move through the birds' rookeries like bulls in a china shop, crushing nests, eggs, and slow-moving chicks in the process.

These extremely gregarious, tusked, and bewhiskered symbols of the Arctic seas haul out in vast aggregations on ice and on certain rocky islands in the Bering and Chukchi seas. The upper canines in both sexes have developed into long white tusks, which are used as head props, defensive weapons, ice picks, probes to find food, and a fifth limb to "tooth-walk" onto the ice. Their most important function, however, is to convey status—the biggest walrus with the biggest tusks tends to be the most dominant. Male Pacific walrus can reach lengths of ten feet or more and weigh up to a ton. Walrus breed in January and February during the coldest part of the winter. During this time, breeding bulls engage in incessant vocal displays which have been compared in function to the repetitive territorial calls of birds. The sexes segregate seasonally. Bulls congregate in separate haul-out and feeding areas in the Bering Sea during spring, while the cows and most of the immature animals migrate northward into the Chukchi Sea. The sexes remain separate throughout the summer, rejoining when the females return to the Bering Sea in the fall. Segregating this way, Pacific walrus minimize the potential conflict between adult and adolescent males in the breeding season as well as distribute their impact on the food supply.

85 WESTERN SANDPIPERS *Calidris mauri*

86   WHITE-BEARDED GNU or WILDEBEEST   *Connochaetes taurinus albojubatus*

142

87 WHITE-BEARDED GNU or WILDEBEEST *Connochaetes taurinus albojubatus* GRANT'S ZEBRA *Equus burchelli böhmi*

Masai Mara Game Reserve, Kenya

88   WHITE-BEARDED GNU or WILDEBEEST   *Connochaetes taurinus albojubatus*

144

Sandpipers, affectionately called "teeter-tails" for their head-bobbing gait, are members of the most diverse family of shorebirds. Worldwide there are more than eighty species of small to medium-sized birds in the sandpiper family, including curlews, sanderlings, snipes, godwits, and dowitchers. It is said that the entire world population of breeding western sandpipers depends on Alaska's Copper River Delta as a staging area during their spring migration to the Arctic. As they gather each year to rest and refuel before heading further north to their breeding areas, it is possible to hear the roar of 30,000 of these inconspicuous one-ounce birds. Similarly, the Western population of dunlin, or red-backed sandpipers, also depends on this vital migratory resource. The delta is the largest coastal wetland in the Pacific Northwest, encompassing 700,000 acres of varying habitat. In May 1990, portions of it were dedicated as part of the Western Hemisphere Shorebird Reserve Network—a designation which indicates that more than one million birds pass through this critical migratory staging area. As many as 20 million birds use the delta each year.

Both species of sandpipers are hardly larger than sparrows. They use their two-inch-long bills to probe the tidal flats in search of mollusks, crustaceans, and insects. During their winter migration, sandpipers are often seen in flocks by the hundreds. When disturbed, they fly up and dart away over the surf, flying so closely, just inches apart, that they look like a flying carpet as they twist and turn over the shoreline. Sandpipers migrating along the eastern United States stop at James Bay, Ontario, to build up fat reserves to fuel their flights to winter refuges in Central and South America. Some double their weight in three weeks on a diet of mollusks and insects.

Like the canary in the coal mine, the presence or absence of birds in an environment is an indication of the overall health of that environment. A sandy beach without a flock of shorebirds chasing the surf seems somehow empty. But should a flock of sandpipers suddenly erupt into the air, you can bet a raptor is near. Peregrine falcons can swoop down at 200 miles per hour to pick off a sandpiper. Because a flock of birds has many eyes and ears for finding food and spotting predators, flock members are less likely to be caught by such a raptor—especially when the flock engages in rapid predator evasion. To thwart an aerial attack, sandpipers close their ranks and "ball up," quickly changing flight direction. This makes it difficult for a falcon to pluck an individual bird from the flock. Flying at such high speeds, falcons will not attempt to dive through a flock and risk injury, so each time the sandpipers ball up, the predator is forced to abort its attack and try again, or fly away. Because their ability to forage, evade predators, and migrate is so critical to their survival, shorebirds molt their flight feathers in sequence, not all at once, which allows them to continue flying all year long. Dull-colored winter plumage, darker above and lighter below, enables them to absorb heat from the sun while spending less energy in predator avoidance.

Similar to a group of Adélie penguins hesitant to enter the water for fear of a chance encounter with a voracious leopard seal, milling wildebeest are reluctant to enter the swift currents and crocodile-infested waters of Kenya's Mara River. Finally, after much crowding, bellowing, and sparring, the animals at the edge of the river are pushed in, and the rest of the herd promptly follows. Each year, wildebeest follow a 500-mile clockwise migration from the southeastern Serengeti plains to the western woodlands, then north to Kenya's Masai Mara. By the time the herds return with the rains to the Serengeti, they will have covered at least 1,000 miles. By allowing large areas of vegetation time to regenerate, this pattern of rotating migration helps max-imize the number of grazers the land can support. American cattle ranchers use a similar technique of pasture rotation to preserve their grazing areas.

A murmuring, grunting wall of migrating wildebeest drowns out all other sounds. At 350 pounds per animal, the combined weight of 300,000 animals moving through an eight-square-mile valley is about 52,500 tons. This aggregation of grass-eating mam-mals leaves the open plains along their route cropped close as if trimmed by a giant lawnmower. The wildebeest then disperse in scattered groups across hundreds of square miles of western woodlands. Six months later when the rains return, they will congregate to munch their way across the grasslands once again.

With legs splayed and bodies arched, wildebeest make acrobatic leaps off the high banks of the Mara River to free-fall and then belly flop into the brown water below. Most traditional wildebeest crossings along the Mara seem to have easy access into the river, but not out of it, and many animals get trapped in the water by the steep, eroded banks on the other side. Crushed and drowned, the weak, young, and old often do not survive to see greener plains. As many as 10,000 in two weeks succumb to the waters of the Mara. Their contorted, bloated bodies litter the river, providing a rigor-mortis feast for maribou storks, vultures, and crocodiles.

Tanzania's Serengeti National Park protects roughly half of a grassland ecosystem that feeds over two million plains mammals—the largest such congregation on Earth. Kenya's Masai Mara marks the northern portion of this 9,600-square-mile area as well as the northern limits of an annual migration that takes vast herds of wildebeest, gazelle, and zebra on a clockwise route in search of seasonal food and water. Increasing competition for these critical resources threatens Africa's wildlife and the parks that protect them. Because cattle convey wealth and status to those who own them, there is cultural pressure for families to own as many as possible. Yet unlike Africa's native antelope, cattle need more water, tear up grass by the roots, and leave the earth trampled into hard-packed wasteland, especially around water-holes. During times of drought, they leave little vegetation to regenerate, causing both livestock and wildlife to starve.

Dendrocygna viduata WHITE-FACED WHISTLING DUCKS

Dendrocygna autumnalis BLACK-BELLIED WHISTLING DUCKS   **91**

Masai Mara Game Reserve, Kenya

90   WHITE-BEARDED GNU or WILDEBEEST   *Connochaetes taurinus albojubatus*

92 WHOOPER SWANS *Cygnus cygnus*

Honshu, Japan

93 WHOOPER SWANS *Cygnus cygnus* NORTHERN PINTAILS *Anas acuta*

Honshu, Japan

94 WHOOPER SWANS *Cygnus cygnus* NORTHERN PINTAILS *Anas acuta*

90 WHITE-BEARDED GNU or WILDEBEEST *Connochaetes taurinus albojubatus* .... Masai Mara Game Reserve, Kenya

It has been said that the gnu, or wildebeest, has "the forequarters of an ox, the hindquarters of an antelope, and the tail of a horse." Their name, *gnu*, is derived from the Hottentot word '*t*' *gnu*, which describes their loud bellowing snort. These large bearded antelope are unusual in more ways than in just their name and anatomy. Wildebeest are picky eaters and prefer only a few species of grasses—at certain heights—and they choose range where waterholes are infrequent, even though they need to drink more water than most grazing species. Females synchronize their births, grouping together to produce as many as twenty calves per hour. They give birth standing up—kneeling only on their front knees—to literally drop their calves onto the plains.

91 WHITE-FACED WHISTLING DUCKS *Dendrocygna viduata* BLACK-BELLIED WHISTLING DUCKS *Dendrocygna autumnalis* Llanos Plains, Venezuela

Thought to be allied most closely with geese and swans, the nine species of whistling ducks form a distinctive group. They have been nicknamed the "tree ducks," because certain species, such as the black-bellied whistling duck of the American tropics, nest in tree cavities. All species are native to tropical and subtropical regions. They feed mainly on plants but will also eat mollusks and crustaceans. Long-necked and long-legged, their hunched backs and broad-winged flight profiles help reveal their identity—as do their namesake whistling calls, which they produce while in flight or perched in trees.

92 WHOOPER SWANS *Cygnus cygnus* .... Hokkaido, Japan

Whooper swans are famous for their loud, bugling calls. While vocalizing, they repeat their resonant *hoo-hoo-hoo* call up to a dozen times. This behavior has earned them the reputation of being the noisiest wild swans in the world. Whooper swans breed from Iceland across Eurasia along seacoasts, rivers, and lakes. Most of the eastern population migrates to the Japanese islands of Honshu and Hokkaido to pass the winter months. Others cross the Bering Strait to winter in the Aleutian and Pribilof islands.

At one time Icelanders believed that whooper swans possessed supernatural powers. At the end of the breeding season, the swans were thought to fly off to the moon.

Lying on the ground in a tight flock, with their heads tucked under their wings, the white geese do literally disappear under a light blanket of drifting snow.

Because whooper swans usually feed in deeper water than the dabbling northern pintails, the two species do not compete for food. Instead, when the swans use their long necks to pull up aquatic plants from deeper waters, they actually help to make additional floating food available to the ducks.

Each year several hundred species of birds migrate hundreds of thousands of miles following the same traditional flyways. Fidelity to place is an interesting concept. In German, it is referred to as *Ortstrue*, meaning the tendency of individuals to return to the places used by their ancestors. They return in order to feed, to reproduce, or simply just to rest. The fixed migration routes of many different species of birds and animals best illustrate this phenomenon. Migratory animals stop at the same resting and refueling places en route to the same breeding and overwintering sites used by their ancestors. In many cases, the same nests and breeding territories are used by one generation after another.

Hokkaido, Japan

96   WHOOPER SWANS *Cygnus cygnus*

Cygnus cygnus WHOOPER SWANS   97

Hokkaido, Japan

Whooper swans migrate both by day and by night. Like most birds, they use the position of the sun to tell them where they are during the day, and the position of the stars in the sky to guide them at night. It is thought that birds also navigate using low-frequency sound waves, polarized light, the Earth's magnetic field, and winds and smells. An internal clock tells the birds when to migrate, and an internal compass tells them where to go. How they keep time remains a mystery. Because migration flights are usually long and exhausting, many birds follow direct and unobstructed flyways over oceans or along coastlines and mountain ranges. Fifteen major avian flyways from breeding grounds to wintering areas have been identified around the globe.

There are seven species of swans in the world, five of which are pure white. Swans are the largest of all waterfowl, a group that also includes ducks and geese. The males, or *cobs*, and the females, or *pens*, both participate in much head-to-head posturing and mutual bill-dipping during courtship. Because of their great size and long wings, swans must run across the water surface in order to get airborne. Once aloft, they fly with slow wing beats, often at great heights in V-formation. During long-distance migrations, waterfowl fly high and fast at altitudes approaching five miles and at speeds in excess of fifty miles per hour. As a result, many migratory birds compete with planes for air space. One nighttime collision between an airplane and a flock of wild swans caused severe damage to the plane but no human casualties. Other bird-plane collisions have resulted in crashes and fatalities.

Like animal tracks in snow indicating the invisible presence of nocturnal wildlife, or Peru's mysterious Nazca Lines left by an unknown people, the passage of countless hooves across a dry expanse in Amboseli National Park leaves an artistic impression of the never-ending quest for food and water.

1 ADÉLIE PENGUINS *Pygoscelis adeliae* .... Paulet Island, Antarctica
200-400mm zoom, f/16 at 1/60 second, Fujichrome 100
Rush hour on a frozen lake, Adélie penguins march to the sea. Pleased with the oncoming perspective, I fixed a direct angle on these tuxedoed birds from an adjacent hillside.

2 AFRICAN ELEPHANTS *Loxodonta africana* .... Amboseli National Park, Kenya
80-200mm zoom, f/8 at 1/250 second, Fujichrome Velvia
Every morning the elephants descend from the higher scrubland to waterholes in Amboseli. In spite of their immense size, the elephants' coloring allows them to completely disappear into the soft taupe hues of the arid landscape. We flew back and forth along the foothills of Mt. Kilimanjaro looking for the clouds of dust that mark their passage. We were often misled by Masai goat and cattle herds, which also kicked up dust on the boundaries of the park.

3 AFRICAN ELEPHANTS *Loxodonta africana* .... Etosha National Park, Namibia
200-400mm zoom, f/8 at 1/125 second, Fujichrome Velvia
After waiting in our vehicle for two hours in the hot afternoon desert, we noticed a cloud of dust rising in the distance above the trees. Within moments an entire herd of elephants appeared pounding straight toward us, converging at the waterhole.

4 AFRICAN OPENBILLS *Anastomus lamelligerus* .... Okavango Delta, Botswana
200-400mm zoom, f/4 at 1/25 second, Fujichrome Velvia
Shooting into the west to obtain the most light, I was able to photograph these spiraling birds at a shutter speed fast enough to stop the motion of their flight. Lifted by warm thermal currents, the openbills soared across the sunset.

5 AMERICAN ALLIGATORS *Alligator mississippiensis* .... The Everglades, Florida
80-200mm zoom, f/16 at 1/15 second, Fujichrome Velvia
The twisting, writhing alligators in this nest were woven into a reptilian tapestry. I was intrigued by their primeval shapes and intertwined bodies.

6 ANCIENT BUSHMEN ROCK CARVINGS .... Twyfelfonstein region, West Central Namibia
50mm macro, f/16 at 1/15 second, Fujichrome Velvia
Estimated to be 2,000 years old, these chiseled rock carvings depict herds of animals in motion across the ancient plains of Namibia.

7 AMERICAN WOOD STORKS *Mycteria americana* .... Hato el Frio, Llanos Plains, Venezuela
200-400mm zoom, f/11 at 1/25 second, Fujichrome Velvia
Since the rookery where I took this photo is located on a privately owned ranch, the birds had grown accustomed to the presence of livestock and people. Consequently, I was able to walk right up to the edge of their nesting place to shoot. More than 2,000 wood storks had congregated at this Venezuelan rookery—creating an abundant food source for hungry predators. Crested caracaras patrolled the rookery's edge, and ocelot tracks marked the passage of a hunting feline. The wood storks are quite vulnerable as they roost in mangrove trees that grow along a narrow area of the stream.

8 BALD EAGLES *Haliaeetus leucocephalus* .... Southeast Alaska
200-400mm zoom, f/16 at 1/4 second, Fujichrome Velvia
Every fall, up to 3,000 eagles congregate on the banks of the Chilkat River to feed on spawned-out salmon. Since bald eagles are typically portrayed in lofty solo flight or perched regally on high pinnacles, it was strange to see these symbols of nobility and strength grounded and hunkered over the last vestiges of dead fish. The clarity of the single eagle in the center magnifies the feeding frenzy of the other birds.

9 BAT STARS *Patiria miniata* .... Queen Charlotte Islands, British Columbia, Canada
50mm macro, f/11 at 1/8 second, Fujichrome 100
Wading through the shallow tide pools of the Queen Charlotte Islands, I came upon this colorful gathering of bat stars. Never before had I seen such a remarkable combination of vibrant hues in the wild. Since this book is not only a collection of migrations, but also of art based on nature, I felt compelled to include this perfect example of patterns of both color and shape.

10 BELUGA WHALES *Delphinapterus leucas* .... Somerset Island, Canadian Arctic
80-200mm zoom, f/4 at 1/250 second, Fujichrome 100
I made arrangements with the Canadian Wildlife Department to fly above these beluga whales long before I departed for Canada. When the day arrived, we circled over the whales in a twin-otter plane. The pilot skillfully slowed the aircraft to sixty miles per hour, allowing me to get this shot. Above the shoreline of Somerset Island in the Canadian Arctic, an aerial perspective confirmed the arrival of nearly two thousand whales, a number impossible to witness from sea level.

11 BLACK-BROWED ALBATROSS *Diomedea melanophrys*
ROCKHOPPER PENGUINS *Eudyptes chrysocome* .... Falkland Islands
200-400mm zoom, f/22 at 1/15 second, Fujichrome Velvia
Loathe to leave their vulnerable chicks unguarded, albatross parents perch atop their nests made of packed mud. Interspersed among the albatross, rockhopper penguins are dwarfed by the elevated network. Unlike many other albatross species of this region, the black-browed albatross nest close together. They reminded me of flamingos in their ability to construct neat nests out of the surrounding mud. I could walk around the edge of the rookery without disturbing them.

12 BLACK-NECKED STILTS *Himantopus mexicanus* .... Llanos Plains, Venezuela
200-400mm zoom, f/16 at 1/125 second, Fujichrome Velvia
The distinctive black-and-white markings and graceful contour of these birds made them great subject matter. In strong winds, it appeared as if they landed and took off in slow motion, their long legs dangling behind.

13 BURCHELL'S ZEBRAS *Equus burchelli* .... Etosha National Park, Namibia
200-400mm zoom, f/11 at 1/125 second, Fujichrome Velvia
Driven by thirst, these wary zebras came out of the surrounding scrubland to drink at the waterhole during the warmest part of the day. They ventured from cover when the light was most intense, presenting a challenge in gauging exposures. I like the view of looking straight on at all the stripes, heads, and eyes of these watchful drinkers.

14 CAPE BUFFALO *Syncerus caffer caffer* .... Amboseli National Park, Kenya
80-200mm zoom, f/2.8 at 1/500 second, Fujichrome
From the outset of this project, I visualized an image such as this one, capturing the force, power, and primeval drive of wildlife. Flying above the park in a microlight aircraft, we were thrilled to happen upon this stampeding herd, thundering across the dusty expanse of the Amboseli plain.

15 CAPE FUR SEALS *Arctocephalus pusillus* .... Cape Cross, Namibia
80-200mm zoom, f/22 at 1/15 second, Fujichrome
The seemingly lifeless landscape of the Namibian coast abuts the cold waters of the South Atlantic, which is teeming with marine life. The stark contrast between the two is abrupt. The water is very cold, the landscape very hot. On the thin margin between the two, nearly 100,000 Cape fur seals congregate. My goal was to convey the pattern and density created by these beached seals. The trick was to capture as many seals in focus as I possibly could without sacrificing the sense of scale.

16 CAPE FUR SEALS *Arctocephalus pusillus* .... Cape Cross, Namibia
80-200mm zoom, f/22 at 1/15 second, Fujichrome Velvia
Thousands of seals were bathed in a golden glow preceding sunset as cormorants flew along the shore. This wealth of wildlife appeared in stark contrast to the high sand dunes and arid landscape surrounding the seal colony.

17 CHINSTRAP PENGUINS *Pygoscelis antarctica* .... South Georgia Island
200-400mm zoom, f/16 at 1/30 second, Fujichrome Velvia

These penguins are not afraid of people, so when I quietly walked around the edge of their rookery, they did not move. Still, they were difficult to photograph. With little light it was a challenge to get the greatest depth of field. Unlike the other penguin rookeries I have photographed, there was no vantage point that would have given me the pattern and perspective of height. I had to rely on a much smaller depth of field to compress the scene.

18 CARIBOU *Rangifer tarandus* .... Brooks Range, Alaska
200-400mm zoom, f/11 at 1/60 second, Fujichrome 100

While floating down the Hula Hula River in the Arctic National Wildlife Refuge, we had a chance encounter with a portion of the great Porcupine caribou herd. We saw no caribou the first four days, and then one appeared on the horizon, and within minutes, hundreds came into view. Within an hour there formed one of the greatest wildlife spectacles I've ever seen. Hooves clicking in constant movement, a plethora of caribou dappled the summer-green tundra. We witnessed some 30,000 animals move through and pass out of sight within hours. This image is just a small vignette of the overall greater herd.

19 CREVALLE JACK FISH *Caranx hippos* .... Crystal River, Florida
Nikonos 20mm wide-angle, f/4 at 1/125 second, Fujichrome 100

I was confronted by a wall of silver as I photographed this mass of synchronized movement. The Crystal River hosts these jack fish every winter. Fed by the warmer waters of many surrounding springs, it serves as an ideal escape from the cool waters of the Gulf of Mexico.

20 ELEGANT TERNS *Sterna elegans* .... Isla de Rasa, Mexico
80-200mm, f/22 at 1/15 second, Fujichrome Velvia

Filling the frame from corner to corner with terns displays the strong repetition of shapes throughout and illustrates how the pattern becomes the subject.

21 ELK or WAPITI *Cervus elaphus* .... National Elk Refuge, Wyoming
80-200mm zoom, f/8 at 1/125 second, Fujichrome 50

Long shadows cast by the low winter sun populated a snowy field with spectral images of elk. In an attempt to capture the longest shadows, I made arrangements to photograph from a helicopter just before sunset. Joined by a biologist, we were able to assess their behavior and maneuver around the herd without disturbing the animals.

22 ELK or WAPITI *Cervus elaphus* .... Yellowstone National Park, Wyoming
200-400mm zoom, f/5.6 at 1/125 second, Fujichrome Velvia

Snow, like fog, diffuses detail, which enabled me to paint a softer interpretation of the elk moving into the wind-whipped snow.

23 EMPEROR PENGUINS *Aptenodytes forsteri* .... Halley Bay, Antarctica
200-400mm zoom, f/11 at 1/15 second, Fujichrome Velvia

These penguins were nesting on frozen sea ice on top of a glacier in early November. I climbed up through the glacier to the top of a 300-foot ice cliff in order to get an aerial view of the birds.

24 ELK or WAPITI *Cervus elaphus* .... National Elk Refuge, Wyoming
80-200mm zoom, f/8 at 1/125 second, Fujichrome 50

The most successful perspective from which to display patterns is from the air. Aerials create a more dynamic composition and provide a pattern otherwise absent from the ground.

25 GEMSBOKS *Oryx gazella* .... Etosha National Park, Namibia
200-400mm zoom, f/8 at 1/25 second, Fujichrome Velvia

I photographed these animals from an underground blind built by biologists. Constructed to sustain the weight of the heaviest bull elephant, the concrete blind provided a cool shelter from the searing heat. Sensing but not seeing me, these wary gemsboks were reluctant to put their heads down to drink. Watchful at this waterhole, they lined up to drink under the sweltering Namibian sky. The symmetrical black lines sophisticate these animals, distinguishing them from the muddy ruggedness of the wildebeest and buffalo.

26 GRANT'S ZEBRAS *Equus burchelli böhmi* .... Masai Mara Game Reserve, Kenya
200-400mm, f/16 at 1/160 second, Fujichrome Velvia

Designed to confuse a charging predator, the dramatic black-and-white stripes of the zebra herd produce an optical illusion. Whereas the dark-colored wildebeest stand out against the vegetation, an entire herd of zebras can disappear in the cryptic confusion of light and dark. From a distance, their black-and-white stripes turn to gray as they vanish in a wavy mirage at the horizon. The play of shape, line, and texture allows the art of the animals to come forward, and the image becomes less a herd of zebras than a movement of lines.

27 GRANT'S ZEBRAS *Equus burchelli böhmi* .... Masai Mara Game Reserve, Kenya
200-400mm zoom, f/11 at 1/250 second, Fujichrome Velvia

While driving through the plains of East Africa, we would often see ungulates in the distance such as zebra or wildebeest, all standing and staring intently in the same direction. Resembling hunting dogs on point, a herd of zebra signaled the presence of danger. This was often our first clue to the presence of predators such as lions and leopards.

28 GREAT WHITE PELICANS *Pelecanus onocrotalus* .... Lake Nakuru, Kenya
800mm, f/5.6 at 1/60 second, Fujichrome Velvia

I found that if I lowered the camera angle, keeping my head level with those of the pelicans, it was possible to reveal the mirrored image of this gentle grouping. The soft light, the reflection of the ivory birds, and the complementary color scheme of orange and blue combine to give this image a sense of serenity.

29 GREATER SANDHILL CRANES *Grus canadensis* Bosque del Apache National Wildlife Refuge, New Mexico
800mm, f/8 at 1/500 second, Fujichrome Velvia

More graceful in the air than on the ground, sandhill cranes wing with seemingly effortless speed. Photographing these birds in autumn offered a variety of artistic options. In the late-afternoon light, I panned as the cranes flew from the cornfields to roost.

30 GREATER SANDHILL CRANES *Grus canadensis* Bosque del Apache National Wildlife Refuge, New Mexico
200-400mm zoom, f/5.6 at 1/250 second, Fujichrome Velvia

Like pelicans and storks, the sandhill cranes circle in groups on invisible air currents. I have seen them flying over Denali National Park, only to slow and suddenly form into a tight spiral to save energy.

31 GREEN SEA TURTLES *Chelonia mydas* .... Galapagos Islands, Ecuador
50mm macro, f/8 at 1/30 second, Kodachrome 64

Braving air attacks from frigate birds and gulls, these vulnerable hatchlings struggled across the sand to the sea. Lapping waves gently ushered them into the more hospitable marine environment. I took a reading off the sand during late-afternoon light to capture the dark detailing of the turtles' shells.

32 HONEYBEES *Apis mellifera* .... Western Washington
50mm macro, f/16 with flash, Fujichrome 50

Transforming pollen into nectar in hexagonal wax cells, drones labor at a feverish pace. The bees proved to be a versatile subject, and in this image I experimented with the effect created by two flash units which picked up the translucent structure of the wings.

33 HUMPBACK WHALES *Megaptera novaeangliae* .... Frederick Sound, Alaska
200-400mm zoom, f/8 at 1/125 second, Fujichrome 100

Like our search in Kenya for dust clouds to identify cryptic elephant herds, in Alaska we searched for spume, the exhaled breath of the humpback whale. Humpback whales exhale geysers of salty mist as they skim the surface of the quiet morning waters. It is remarkable to see humpbacks in the wild, because even though they are sometimes forty feet long and weigh forty tons, all that is visible is their small dorsal fin and occasionally a tail.

34 IMPALAS *Aepyceros melampus* .... Masai Mara Game Reserve, Kenya

200-400mm zoom, f/8 at 1/125 second, Fujichrome 50

Moving as one, this graceful herd of impalas traveled across the grassy plains of the Mara River region. Impalas are difficult to photograph, because if one animal decides to leave, they all leave. What I like about this shot, as in so many throughout this collection, is the strong directional flow of the animals.

35 IMPERIAL SHAGS *Phalacrocorax atriceps* .... Falkland Islands

80-200mm zoom, f/16 at 1/60 second, Fujichrome Velvia

Gullets engorged with fish for their hungry young, blue-eyed shags march en masse to their nesting ground. Because they have never been hunted by humans, they were remarkably tame and quite approachable. They would land just a few feet away, oblivious to their human observers.

36 KING PENGUINS *Aptenodytes patagonicus* .... South Georgia Island

50mm macro, f/22 at 1/15 second, Fujichrome 50

I took this photo in the middle of the day when the light was overcast, allowing the subtleties of the penguins' white and orange feathers to be distinguished. Under bright light, the white of the birds is so glaring that it can overwhelm the film and make the color distinctions less dramatic.

37 INDIANA BATS *Myotis sodalis* .... Ozarks, Arkansas

50mm macro, f/22 with flash, Fujichrome Velvia

To get this shot, I crawled three-fourths of a mile on my knees with a backpack that scraped the cave ceiling. It was in the middle of winter and very cold. The cave opened up into a larger chamber where approximately 5,000 hibernating bats hung from the ceiling just five feet above the floor. I was allowed into the cave with biologist Michael Harvey, who conducts a census once every winter. Because the heat from our bodies could wake the tiny two-inch bats from their winter slumber, putting them at risk in the cold temperatures, we had to work fast. I was permitted to shoot only one roll of film in a ten-minute period. Dr. Harvey quickly counted the bats using a yardstick that he held near their heads, calculating three hundred bats per square foot. I photographed them with a macro lens and two flash units while bending backward under the low cave ceiling.

I like this image because it takes a while to realize that you are looking at little bat noses and mouths. It is such a tight shot that it becomes an abstract.

38 KING PENGUINS *Aptenodytes patagonicus* .... Royal Bay, South Georgia Island

200-400mm zoom, f/16 at 1/30 second, Fujichrome Velvia

I had been after this image for a long time. "Woolies" are the chicks from the previous season. They live a whole year on the beach in feathers that look like velvet. A host of king penguin chicks bask in the subantarctic sun of South Georgia Island. The golden auras of the afternoon light frame only the chicks in this sweeping panorama.

39 KING PENGUINS *Aptenodytes patagonicus* .... South Georgia Island

200-400mm zoom, f/16 at 1/30 second, Fujichrome Velvia

To create this abstract pattern with woolies, I carefully maneuvered myself to take full advantage of the backlighting. It was difficult to focus because their fuzzy feathers were blowing in the breeze. I finally had to concentrate on the sharp lines of their beaks in order to shoot the birds in focus. These adolescent penguins were surprisingly fearless and gregarious. I would set up my camera to shoot a pattern, only to have the pattern disrupted as the birds approached me to investigate. I had to work very quickly, literally hiding from them in order to get this picture.

40 KING PENGUINS *Aptenodytes patagonicus* .... South Georgia Island

200-400mm zoom, f/22 at 1/15 second, Fujichrome Velvia

It was necessary to stop down the camera to get the penguins in focus since they were spanning such a large area. By gaining height, I managed a greater depth of field.

41 KING PENGUINS *Aptenodytes patagonicus* .... South Georgia Island

80-200mm zoom, f/22 at 1/8 second, Fujichrome Velvia

The king penguins held tightly together during a blowing gale. Their otherwise slick pattern was broken by their shaggy, rough, molting feathers.

42 LADYBIRD BEETLES *Hippodamia convergens* .... White Horse, Washington

50mm macro, f/4 with flash, Fujichrome 100

Standing on the craggy peaks of the Cascades, I was taken in by the vast panoramas. I glanced down to discover a tiny, thriving colony at my feet. Living cloisonné, ladybugs swarmed in the stony crevices.

43 LESSER FLAMINGOS *Phoenicopterus minor* .... Lake Magadi, Rift Valley, Kenya

80-200mm zoom, f/2.8 at 1/500 second, Fujichrome Velvia

As we flew close to this gathering of birds, the small, quiet engines of the custom-built microlight caused little disturbance to the flock. Only their shadows revealed their true identity—that of flamingos. Their long legs and gracefully curved necks appeared as if painted on the mud flats of Lake Magadi.

44 LESSER FLAMINGOS *Phoenicopterus minor* .... Lake Magadi, Rift Valley, Kenya

80-200mm zoom, f/2.8 at 1/500 second, Fujichrome Velvia

I photographed these flamingos as they sprinted across the shallow lake to gain momentum for flight. Gliding above them in the microlight, I concentrated solely on perspective, hoping that the young French pilot knew what he was doing. It was only after we landed safely that he confessed to visual disorientation during the flight. Banking at steep angles while mesmerized by the sheer magnitude and movement of the flock, his sense of height and horizon was frequently distorted.

45 LESSER FLAMINGOS *Phoenicopterus minor* .... Lake Magadi, Rift Valley, Kenya

80-200mm zoom, f/2.8 at 1/500 second, Fujichrome Velvia

Although the flamingos in this image look as if they are flying parallel to the water, they are actually rising steeply from the lake, sweeping up at a sharp angle. As we followed the flamingos in the microlight, I was completely captivated by this avian spectacle and shot as many rolls of film as I could. The drama of the scene was intensified by the sharp contrast between the birds' brilliant pink legs and the dark green water.

46 LESSER FLAMINGOS *Phoenicopterus minor* .... Lake Magadi, Rift Valley, Kenya

80-200mm zoom, f/2.8 at 1/500 second, Fujichrome Velvia

Flamingos migrate up and down the Rift Valley as the water levels change, creating dramatic visual patterns as they fly en masse. This shot was taken from the microlight in the cool calm of early morning. I caught the birds as they flew over a reflection of the clouds that drifted above us. Later in the day, when the temperatures soared to 100 degrees Fahrenheit, thermal turbulence made flying and photography virtually impossible.

47 LESSER FLAMINGOS *Phoenicopterus minor* .... Lake Magadi, Rift Valley, Kenya

80-200mm zoom, f/2.8 at 1/500 second, Fujichrome Velvia

Accompanied by their shadows, a flock of flamingos skims the surface of Lake Magadi. Like a mirror, the glassy surface reflected the sky so perfectly that we lost track of the boundary between water and air. It wasn't until we saw the reflection of our faces in the lake that we realized how close to the surface we had flown.

48 LESSER FLAMINGOS *Phoenicopterus minor* .... Lake Magadi, Rift Valley, Kenya

800mm, f/5.6 at 1/250 second, Fujichrome Velvia

Unlike the other flamingo shots, this photograph was taken from land on a rocky outcrop along the shore. I panned with a long lens as the graceful birds slowly flew by.

49 LESSER FLAMINGOS *Phoenicopterus minor* .... Lake Magadi, Rift Valley, Kenya
80-200mm zoom, f/2.8 at 1/500 second, Fujichrome Velvia

It was difficult to imagine that such a dry, desolate area could support any life at all. Yet as we approached Lake Magadi from the air, we suddenly discovered that it was teeming with colorful birds. The strata of flamingos lifted in waves across the shallows of the lake.

50 LESSER FLAMINGOS *Phoenicopterus minor* .... Lake Nakuru, Kenya
800mm, f/11 at 1/25 second, Fujichrome Velvia

Seeking a more intimate perspective of the flamingos, I lay in the mud at the lake's edge, quietly waiting for them to move closer. Sweeping back and forth in tight formation, the flamingos created a sea of perpetual pink movement.

51 LESSER FLAMINGOS *Phoenicopterus minor* .... Lake Magadi, Rift Valley, Kenya
800mm, f/16 at 1/25 second, Fujichrome Velvia

Crowding in for a drink of fresh water, vermilion-accented flamingos swarm toward a stream feeding the alkaline waters of Lake Magadi. To attain maximum detail, I situated myself on a cliff above the flock. This allowed for a closer study of the birds.

52 LONG-BILLED DOWITCHERS *Limnodromus scolopaceus* Bosque del Apache National Wildlife Refuge, New Mexico
800mm, f/16 at 1/60 second, Fujichrome Velvia

Using a telephoto lens and a long exposure, I compressed the image to bring the foreground and the distant birds into focus. This is an uncharacteristically still shot of these birds mirrored in the royal blue shallows and lingering in the warmth of the morning sun.

53 MALLARD DUCKS *Anas platyrhynchos* George C. Reifel Migratory Bird Sanctuary, British Columbia, Canada
50mm macro, f/16 at 1 second, Fujichrome Velvia

To create a sense of play and motion, the use of a long exposure became essential. I like this image simply because the ducks' webbed feet are so sharp in contrast to the blurred action. Forever moving, these mallard ducks busy themselves in search of food.

54 MALLARD DUCKS *Anas platyrhynchos* .... Stanley Park, British Columbia, Canada
50mm macro, f/16 at 2 seconds, Fujichrome Velvia

Ducks, in their constant stir of activity, provide a perfect subject for this photographic expression. The background palette of aqua offers a tranquil contrast to their brisk movement.

55 MALLARD DUCKS *Anas platyrhynchos* George C. Reifel Migratory Bird Sanctuary, British Columbia, Canada
80-200mm zoom, f/8 at 1/8 second, Fujichrome Velvia

I have always been drawn to impressionistic paintings, to the masters who portrayed their subjects in a very soft haze rather than outlining them precisely. Without detailing every feature, they captured the essence of form. That is what I have attempted to do in many images in this collection. In this example the mallards' color and shape become blurred with their movement, yet they remain distinguishable. As the ducks took flight in the late afternoon light, they virtually painted their ascent across the film.

56 MALLARD DUCKS *Anas platyrhynchos* AMERICAN COOTS *Fulica americana* ....
.... George C. Reifel Migratory Bird Sanctuary, British Columbia, Canada
50mm macro, f/16 at 1/4 second, Fujichrome Velvia

Instead of freezing the frame and bringing all the ducks into sharp focus, the use of a long exposure and correspondingly small f-stop (f/16) allowed me to maximize the movement of the ducks.

57 MALLARD DUCKS *Anas platyrhynchos* George C. Reifel Migratory Bird Sanctuary, British Columbia, Canada
80-200mm zoom, f/16 at 1/30 second, Fujichrome Velvia

In the warm glow of sunrise, these mallard ducks quietly repose on the ice of a frozen lake. The low morning light accentuates the iridescent green heads of the drakes.

58 MONARCH BUTTERFLIES *Danaus plexippus* .... Mexico
200-400mm zoom, f/11 at 1/30 second, Fujichrome 100

Like many other images in this collection, this photograph was carefully planned before I arrived on location. Each fall thousands of monarch butterflies converge on a small patch of forest in the high mountains near Mexico City. Cloaked in metallic orange-and-yellow butterfly wings, the evergreen trees are transformed into a living landscape. Each afternoon as the temperature rose, the butterflies warmed up and began to flutter around. It was impossible to walk through this magical, stirring forest without being covered by butterflies.

59 MUTE SWANS *Cygnus olor* .... Volga Delta, Russia
800mm, f/8 at 1/250 second, Kodachrome 64

Detailed against the steely blue sky, the mute swans took flight over the reedy expanse of the Volga Delta. These swans are extremely wary birds. To see them in large flocks in the wild gave me a new respect for these birds. I had grown accustomed to seeing them in city parks throughout Europe and North America. They are often considered a nuisance in North America, as they displace native North American trumpeter and tundra swans.

60 NORTHERN PINTAILS *Anas acuta* .... Honshu, Japan
50mm macro, f/16 at 1/15 second, Fujichrome 100

Normally frightened by people, these ducks overcome their fear during the harsh winter months to accept the presence of the Japanese farmers who feed them grain. The full light of midday details the texture and color of the birds.

61 NORTHERN GANNETS *Morus bassanus* .... Newfoundland, Canada
200-400mm zoom, f/16 at 1/25 second, Fujichrome 100

Similar to other birds that nest in colonies, northern gannets build their nests at beak's length apart. The nests are comfortably distanced, yet dense enough to allow the birds to thrive in the safety of numbers. This flock was nesting on a smooth plain hundreds of feet above the white-capped waters of the North Atlantic. Overcast conditions enhanced the contrast between the gannets' golden heads and stark white bodies.

62 NORTHERN PINTAILS *Anas acuta* .... Honshu, Japan
20mm wide-angle, f/8 at 1/125 second, Fujichrome 100

The pintails in their haphazard activity and the strident markings of the drakes offered yet another collage of natural design.

63 NORTHERN PINTAILS *Anas acuta* .... Honshu, Japan
80-200mm zoom, f/5.6 at 1/8 second, Fujichrome 100

Huddling in the falling snow, the ducks moved closer and closer together. This image quietly conveys the natural resilience of these little birds.

64 PACIFIC DOUBLE-SADDLE BUTTERFLYFISH *Chaetodon ulietensis* .. Bora Bora, French Polynesia
Nikonos 20mm wide-angle, f/5.6 at 1/125 second, Fujichrome Velvia

I was captivated by the brilliance of the myriad of fish that live in these tropical waters. Suspended in the crystal sea, the butterflyfish hovered in layered symmetry. I was immediately surrounded by a school of these brightly colored fish. The fish, accustomed to being fed by local snorkelers, expected no less from me. It was difficult to get far enough away to photograph them. I ended up swimming as fast and as far away from them as I could, and then waited for them to catch up.

65 PRONGHORN ANTELOPE *Antilocapra americana* .... Yellowstone National Park, Montana
200-400mm zoom, f/11 at 1 second, Fujichrome Velvia

I used a long exposure to create a more painterly image. The only indication of snow in this photograph is the bright reflection off the white underbellies of the loping pronghorn. Reminiscent of a petroglyph, the pronghorns are bounding through snowy, golden grass.

66 RED-BILLED QUELEA *Quelea quelea* .... Okavango Delta, Botswana
800mm, f/5.6 at 1/125 second, Fujichrome 100
Red-billed quelea are under constant attack from raptors, and even the slightest movement startles them into flight. For this reason, I had to photograph them from a vehicle some distance away, using sandbags to steady the long lens.

67 RED-CROWNED CRANES *Grus japonensis* .... Hokkaido, Japan
200-400mm zoom, f/11 at 1/30 second, Fujichrome 100
Periwinkle twilight shrouded the exquisite lines of these lithe birds. Japanese farmers put grain and fish out in their fields, which are located along the flight paths used by the cranes. The cranes come to feed each evening on their way to roost in a nearby swamp for the night. Unlike the zebras and terns, this study in black-and-white presented a challenge because of the snowy backdrop.

68 RED-WINGED BLACKBIRDS *Agelaius phoeniceus* Bosque del Apache National Wildlife Refuge, New Mexico
200-400mm zoom, f/8 at 1/250 second, Fujichrome Velvia
Witnessing this flock of thousands of blackbirds swirl in the air like scattering leaves and then fly directly at us was one of the most dramatic moments of our trip. An explosion of red and black flashes, their red epaulettes were ablaze in the sunlight.

69 RED-WINGED BLACKBIRDS *Agelaius phoeniceus* Bosque del Apache National Wildlife Refuge, New Mexico
200-400mm zoom, f/4 at 1/60 second, Fujichrome Velvia
Concealed in the tall grass, a flock of four or five thousand blackbirds can be completely hidden until they are startled and burst into the air. The presence of predatory sharp-shinned hawks and merlins made them group even tighter. When threatened, the blackbirds appeared to become one bird, a flock of many bodies controlled by a single brain, flying in tight formation.

70 SALTWATER CROCODILES *Crocodylus porosus* .... Borneo
50mm macro, f/16 at 1/15 second, Fujichrome Velvia
Plated in reptilian armor of yellow and black, these crocodiles rest passively in brackish waters. Although this grouping of crocodiles is not a characteristic occurrence, it is a perfect example of the natural design that I am always after.

71 SCARLET IBIS *Eudocimus ruber* .... Caroni Swamp, Trinidad
800mm, f/5.6 at 1 second, Fujichrome 100
These scarlet ibis were one of the more difficult subjects I shot for this book. During the day they scattered out to feed among the shallow mud flats of Trinidad, returning to their roosting trees only at dusk. So precisely did they anticipate sunset that by the time they settled into their sleeping trees, only fifteen minutes of twilight remained before it was too dark to photograph. The difficulty of getting this image was compounded by the lack of dry land from which to film—the roots and trunks of the roosting trees were completely surrounded by water. I created an island using a wooden boat, which I secured to poles sunk deep into the mud. Once stabilized, I used two tripods, one under an 800mm lens and one under the camera body, to take a long, steady exposure of the birds.

72 SCARLET IBIS *Eudocimus ruber* CATTLE EGRETS *Bubulcus ibis* .... Llanos Plains, Venezuela
200-400mm zoom, f/5.6 at 1/15 second, Fujichrome Velvia
During early afternoon the roost was still and empty. Only broken tree limbs hinted at the weight of roosting birds. Near sunset, the stillness was suddenly shattered by an abundance of bird life. I stood dumbfounded as wave after wave of ibis, egrets, and storks in vibrant colors flew in to land in the trees. Jockeying for position, a riotous flock of scarlet and white inundated the mangroves. Because the birds roost only at dusk, very little time was left in which to capture their image before the light was gone.

73 SNOW GEESE *Anser caerulescens* .... Bosque del Apache National Wildlife Refuge, New Mexico
200-400mm zoom, f/8 at 1/4 second, Fujichrome Velvia
This wildlife refuge provided all the classic colors of fall. The ascendant snow geese blazed across the copper and golden reeds of Bosque del Apache, blasting the calm with their beating wings and blaring calls.

74 SNOW GEESE *Anser caerulescens* .... Bosque del Apache National Wildlife Refuge, New Mexico
200-400mm zoom, f/4 at 1/250 second, Fujichrome Velvia
One of the most familiar and recognized wildlife migrations is that of geese. Despite its common occurrence, many aspects of their flight in V-formation remain a mystery. Flying overhead, the snow geese with their characteristic black-tipped wings are showcased dramatically against the deep blue sky.

75 SNOW GEESE *Anser caerulescens* .... Skagit Valley, Washington
80-200mm zoom, f/5.6 at 1/125 second, Fujichrome 100
This aerial shot was taken from a small single-engine plane from which the pilot had removed a window. From this angle it was possible to see the natural design of the marshes below, overlayed by the aerial patterns created by the geese in flight. These are Arctic birds that migrate to Washington from Wrangell Island every October. They stay through March, feeding on the stubble of spent cornfields in the Skagit Valley before returning north to breed.

76 SNOW GEESE *Anser caerulescens* .... Tule Lake, California
800mm, f/5.6 at 1/125 second, Kodachrome 64
Taking flight at once, a myriad of snow geese obscured the mountain range beyond. The eye is easily confused by the multiple layers of birds. I fixed focus on a single bird to capture this photograph.

77 SNOW GEESE *Anser caerulescens* .... Bosque del Apache National Wildlife Refuge, New Mexico
200-400mm zoom, f/11 at 1/30 second, Fujichrome 100
The difficulty of this shot was in gaining the proper exposure to display the distinctions of white on white. This regiment of snow geese, individualized only by their pink bills and black eyes, formed a textured bounty of white.

78 SOCKEYE SALMON *Oncorhynchus nerka* .... Wood River Lakes region, Hansen Creek, Alaska
50mm macro, f/11 at 1/30 second, Fujichrome 100
Consulting the Department of Fisheries at the University of Washington, I determined that the best place in North America to find the brightest spawning salmon was Alaska. The water is the clearest, and the streams are narrow enough to cause the salmon to mass in great numbers. To capture the pattern of these colorful fish, I used a stepladder to gain a slightly different and higher perspective. The salmon formed a solid mass of fish as they struggled to squeeze past barriers created by logs and waterfalls.

79 SOCKEYE SALMON *Oncorhynchus nerka* .... Wood River Lakes region, Hansen Creek, Alaska
80-200mm zoom, f/11 at 1/60 second, Fujichrome 100
From a more traditional angle, I couldn't resist the opportunity to photograph the contrast between the blazing red bodies and jade green heads of these brightly colored fish.

80 SOCKEYE SALMON *Oncorhynchus nerka* .... Wood River Lakes region, Hansen Creek, Alaska
80-200mm zoom, f/8 at 1/60 second, Fujichrome 100
I was able to capture this display of color and pattern by working in the calm of early morning when it was possible to shoot through the surface of the lake. In a small boat, we just drifted among the thousands of salmon congregated at the mouth of the creek, waiting their turn to fight upstream. I used a telephoto lens to photograph them at an angle, letting the sun rays filter through the water to partially illuminate their brilliant colors.

81 SOUTHERN CARMINE BEE-EATERS *Merops nubicoides* .... Okavango Delta, Botswana
200-400mm zoom, f/8 at 1/125 second, Fujichrome Velvia
Anchored in a boat in the Okavango River, I filmed these bee-eaters at their nesting site. The cliffs remained in the shadows throughout the day. The bright sunshine reflected off the water, lighting the muddy walls in soft, even tones. These chalky bluffs provide nests for hundreds of turquoise-splashed carmine bee-eaters.

82 SOUTHERN ELEPHANT SEALS *Mirounga leonina* .... South Georgia Island
80-200mm zoom, f/11 at 1/30 second, Fujichrome Velvia
Although elephant seals are aggressive among themselves, battling for territory and harems, we wandered among them safely. Made lazy and irritable by their annual molt, beached cows barked their annoyance at one another.

83 WALRUS *Odobenus rosmarus* .... Round Island, Alaska
300mm 2.8, f/11 at 1/15 second, Fujichrome 100
Round Island hosts this all-male beach party every summer. With no females present, these comical subjects drop their usual competitive guard and settle in. Working atop a high cliff, I utilized depth of field and perspective to allow the patterns of these large marine mammals to come forward. The overcast light emphasized their varying flesh tones.

84 WESTERN SANDPIPERS *Calidris mauri* **DUNLIN** *Calidris alpina* Bowerman Basin, Grays Harbor, Washington
135mm, f/16 at 1/30 second, Fujichrome 100
I crept within twenty feet of these birds, hoping to get better detail. The early-morning sun cast a warm, rich light on the rusty backs of the sleeping flock.

85 WESTERN SANDPIPERS *Calidris mauri* .... Bowerman Basin, Grays Harbor, Washington
300mm 2.8, f/8 at 1/250 second, Fujichrome 100
I relied on the speed of the shutter to freeze the action and get as many birds into focus as possible.

86 WHITE-BEARDED GNU or WILDEBEEST *Connochaetes taurinus albojubatus* Masai Mara Game Reserve, Kenya
800mm, f/16 at 1/30 second, Fujichrome Velvia
The dust raised by their movements enveloped the wildebeest in an ethereal fog. I was excited by this effect because the fog of dust softened the shapes and created a surrealistic look. The dust helped to distinguish one animal from another, those farthest from the camera appearing to be the softest, lending a depth of field to the image.

87 WHITE-BEARDED GNU or WILDEBEEST *Connochaetes taurinus albojubatus*
GRANT'S ZEBRA *Equus burchelli böhmi* .... Masai Mara Game Reserve, Kenya
600mm, f/16 at 1/30 second, Fujichrome Velvia
The lone zebra engulfed by a sea of moving wildebeest caught my attention. I waited for the instant when the confused zebra turned directly into the herd, and I framed it off-center to add a sense of tension to the image. The eye is drawn straight to the zebra. The fact that the zebra is taller than the wildebeest and standing on a slight knoll accentuates the effect.

88 WHITE-BEARDED GNU or WILDEBEEST *Connochaetes taurinus albojubatus* Masai Mara Game Reserve, Kenya
200-400mm, f/5.6 at 1/250 second, Fujichrome Velvia
The plains of the Serengeti and the Mara River region provide an amazing spectacle of wildlife both in variety and mass. The winding line created by these bleating, thundering mammals as they cross the field of view classically embodies the power and rhythm of migration. The wildebeest enter the image in the foreground to join a pattern created by thousands and thousands of others as they snake toward the horizon. The scale is tremendous, recalling the grandeur and mystique of an earlier age.

89 WHITE-BEARDED GNU or WILDEBEEST *Connochaetes taurinus albojubatus* Masai Mara Game Reserve, Kenya
800mm, f/16 at 1/15 second, Fujichrome Velvia
There are very few places in the world where you can see hundreds of thousands of animals moving together at once. When each animal is the size of a wildebeest, the biomass is quite impressive.

90 WHITE-BEARDED GNU or WILDEBEEST *Connochaetes taurinus albojubatus* Masai Mara Game Reserve, Kenya
200-400mm zoom, f/16 at 1/60 second, Fujichrome Velvia
Because the wildebeest migrate in such incomprehensible numbers, I attempted to portray the feeling of their mass in this photograph.

91 WHITE-FACED WHISTLING DUCKS *Dendrocygna viduata*
BLACK-BELLIED WHISTLING DUCKS *Dendrocygna autumnalis* .... Llanos Plains, Venezuela
200-400mm zoom, f/8 at 1/250 second, Fujichrome Velvia
During the rainy season, the Llanos Plains turn into a huge lake. In the drier months, the water recedes, leaving a few waterholes where thousands of birds congregate to drink. The backdrop of blues and greens offsets the rich brown tones displayed in this assortment of ducks.

92 WHOOPER SWANS *Cygnus cygnus* .... Hokkaido, Japan
80-200mm zoom, f/8 at 1/125 second, Fujichrome 50
The lake was frozen except along the edge where thermal springs flowed down and kept the water free of ice. The birds are wild, spending most of the year in the Siberian Arctic before migrating to Japan. During the winter months when these much-loved birds are fed grain by the devoted Japanese, they quickly lose their fear of people. I used a ladder, as it became clear that in order to feature the number and design of these elegant birds, I would have to get above them.

93 WHOOPER SWANS *Cygnus cygnus* **NORTHERN PINTAILS** *Anas acuta* .... Honshu, Japan
200-400mm zoom, f/11 at 1/60 second, Fujichrome 100
The quiet scene of falling snow details the contrast between the large swans and the hardly identifiable pintails.

94 WHOOPER SWANS *Cygnus cygnus* **NORTHERN PINTAILS** *Anas acuta* .... Honshu, Japan
800mm, f/11 at 1/60 second, Fujichrome 100
In a more traditional view of the lake, the combination of gently blowing snow, beige grasses, snow-blurred lines of tree limbs, and black-and-white birds create the feeling of an impressionistic painting.

95 WHOOPER SWANS *Cygnus cygnus* .... Hokkaido, Japan
20mm wide-angle, f/8 at 1/30 second, Fujichrome 100
Using a wide-angle lens, I was able to bring the whooper swans closer to the foreground, maximizing the depth of field.

96 WHOOPER SWANS *Cygnus cygnus* .... Hokkaido, Japan
200-400mm zoom, f/8 at 1/125 second, Fujichrome 50
Although it was very cold in the early morning when I took this photograph, the swans slept comfortably in the warm steam created by the thermal springs along the shore. Two adults flank their cygnets protectively. The young are born in spring and migrate south from the Arctic to Japan for their first winter.

97 WHOOPER SWANS *Cygnus cygnus* .... Hokkaido, Japan
80-200mm zoom, f/16 at 1/30 second, Fujichrome Velvia
Photographing the swans from a slight elevation captured the diagonal symmetry of their bodies and allowed for a greater depth of field.

98 WILDLIFE TRAILS .... Amboseli National Park, Kenya
80-200mm zoom, f/5.6 at 1/250 second, Fujichrome Velvia
Painting an endless journey of life, the tracks left by thousands of animals are indelibly etched across the dry lake beds of Amboseli.

ACKNOWLEDGMENTS ....

From the photographer:

Special acknowledgment must be made to the many individuals whose assistance, active support, and influence I have relied on to make this book possible. My sincere thanks goes to them and to all those who have contributed to my education and appreciation of wildlife, nature, photography, and art. My heartfelt gratitude to the participants including, but not limited to, those named here.

For their permission and assistance: George C. Reifel Migratory Bird Sanctuary; Bosque del Apache National Wildlife Refuge; Canadian Wildlife Service; National Elk Refuge; and the University of Washington, Department of Fisheries. My personal thanks to: Allstock, Inc.; Argentum Photographic & Digital Services; Ivey-Seright Photo Lab; Peter and Judy Jess, Jessco Operations, Inc.; Gavriel Jecan; Dr. Michael Harvey; Alexis Peltier; Steve Turner, East African Ornithological Tours; Charles Sleicher; and Gary Stolz. Special thanks for the support, research, and talents of my contributing staff: Mel Calvan, Deirdre Skillman, Christine Eckhoff, and Ray Pfortner. For their interest in the subject matter of this book and the generous effort they have granted to its content, design, and overall quality, Beyond Words Publishing, Inc., and Principia Graphica.

From the author:

I would like to acknowledge the following organizations for their significant contributions to this work: *Animals* magazine for the initial assignment, "Migration: Journey of Life," which inspired the research; the Amway Corporation for their interest in promoting public awareness of endangered species; Seattle's Woodland Park Zoo; the American Association of Zoological Parks and Aquariums; the National Audubon Society; Everglades National Park; the J. N. "Ding" Darling National Wildlife Refuge; the U.S. Fish and Wildlife Service; Okefenokee National Wildlife Refuge; Cornell Laboratory of Ornithology; the Rocky Mountain Elk Foundation; Service Argos, Inc.; and the many talents of Beyond Words Publishing, Inc., and Principia Graphica.

The following individuals also deserve special recognition for their assistance: Art Wolfe for the opportunity to write *Migrations*; editor Julie Livingston for the fun, skill, and guidance she brought to the project; Christine Eckhoff and Deirdre Skillman for their technical support and meticulous review of the text; USFWS's Gary Stolz for invaluable fact-checking; fish biologist Murray Schuh for salmon tips; Gretchen Zience for emergency manuscript transportation; my Ph.D. advisor, Dr. Joan Lockard, for her endless encouragement and patience; Bob Citron for much-needed childcare—and for the adventure of having seen most of the animals together in the wild; my parents, Norma and Bill Sleeper, for a lifetime of joy; and my three very patient, animal-loving children, Kelly, David, and Josh Citron, who shared not only the wildlife, but the wild deadlines.

BIBLIOGRAPHY ....

Allen, Gerald R., and Roger C. Steene. *Reef Fishes of the Indian Ocean*. Neptune, N.J.: T.F.H. Publications, 1987.

Ashworth, William. *Penguins, Puffins, and Auks: Their Lives and Behavior*. New York: Crown Publishers, 1993.

Blood, Don, Tom Hall, and Susan Imbaumgarten. *Rocky Mountain Wildlife*. Saanichton, B.C., Canada: Hancock House Publishers, Ltd., 1976.

Brown, L. *The Mystery of the Flamingoes*. London: Hamlyn Publishing Group, Ltd., 1959.

Burton, Robert, ed. *Animal Life*. New York: Oxford University Press, 1991.

Carr, Archie. *So Excellent a Fishe*. Garden City, N.Y.: Natural History Press, 1967.

DiSilvestro, Roger L. *Fight for Survival*. New York: John Wiley & Sons, Inc., 1990.

Dorst, Jean, and Pierre Dandelot. *A Field Guide to the Larger Mammals of Africa*. Great Britain: Collins Publishing, 1978.

Farner, Donald, and James King, eds. *Avian Biology*, vol. II. New York: Academic Press, 1972.

Harrison, George. *Roger Tory Peterson's Dozen Birding Hot Spots*. New York: Simon and Schuster, 1976.

Hauser, Hillay. *Book of Fishes*. Houston, Texas: Gulf Publishing Co., 1984.

Line, Les, Kimball Garrett, and Kenn Kaufman. *The Audubon Society Book of Water Birds*. New York: Harry Abrams, Inc., 1987.

Macdonald, David, ed. *The Encyclopedia of Mammals*. New York: Facts on File Publications, 1984.

McClane, A. J. *McClane's Field Guide to Saltwater Fishes of North America*. New York: Henry Holt & Company, Inc., 1974.

McLachlan, G. R., and R. Liversidge. *Robert's Birds of South Africa*. South Africa: The Trustees of the John Voelcker Bird Book Fund, 1980.

Moyle, Peter B. *Fish: An Enthusiast's Guide*. Berkeley, Calif.: University of California Press, 1993.

Nature's Wonderlands: National Parks of the World. Washington, D.C.: National Geographic Society, 1989.

Page, Jake, and Eugene Morton. *Lords of the Air*. Washington, D.C.: Smithsonian Books, 1989.

Potgieter, Herman, and Clive Walker. *Above Africa: Aerial Photography from the Okavango Swamplands*. New York: Mallard Press, 1989.

Ricketts, Edward, Jack F. Calvin, and Joel W. Hedgpeth. *Between Pacific Tides*. Stanford, Calif.: Stanford University Press, 1968.

Scheffel, Richard, ed. *Nature in America*. Pleasantville, N.Y.: The Reader's Digest Association, Inc., 1991.

Steadman, David, and Steven Zousmer. *Galapagos: Discovery on Darwin's Islands*. Washington, D.C.: Smithsonian Institution Press, 1988.

Terres, John. *The Audubon Society Encyclopedia of North American Birds*. New York: Alfred A. Knopf, 1980.

Willcock, Colin. *Africa's Rift Valley*. Amsterdam: Time-Life International, 1977.

The Wonder of Birds. Washington, D.C.: National Geographic Society, 1983.

The World's Wild Shores. Washington, D.C.: National Geographic Society, 1990.

Wrigley, Robert. *Mammals in North America*. Winnipeg, Manitoba, Canada: Hyperion Press, Ltd., 1986.

Ziesler, Gunter, and Angelika Hofer. *Safari: The East African Diaries of a Wildlife Photographer*. New York: Facts on File Publications, 1984.

RESOURCES ....

To learn more about migratory species and to participate in their conservation, contact the following
organizations:

Adopt-A-Crane Program
International Crane Foundation
P.O. Box 447
Baraboo, WI 53913-0447
608-356-9462

Adopt-An-Acre Program
Platte River Whooping Crane Habitat Maintenance Trust
2550 Diers Ave., Suite H
Grand Island, NE 68803-1214
308-384-4633

American Association of Zoological Parks and
   Aquariums
7970-D Old Georgetown Road
Bethesda, MD 70814
301-907-7777

Defenders of Wildlife
1101 14th St. N.W., Suite 1400
Washington, DC 20005
202-682-9400

National Audubon Society
700 Broadway
New York, NY 10003-9501
1-800-274-4201

National Parks and Conservation Association
1776 Massachussetts Ave. N.W.
Washington, DC 20036
1-800-NAT-PARKS

National Wildlife Federation
8925 Leesburg Pike
Vienna, VA 22184
703-790-4000
1-800-432-6564

The Nature Conservancy
1800 N. Kent St.
Arlington, VA 22209
1-800-628-6860

Neotropical Bird Migration Program
Cornell Laboratory of Ornithology
159 Sapsucker Woods Road
Ithaca, NY 14850
607-254-BIRD

Partners in Flight/Aves de Las Americas
National Fish and Wildlife Foundation
1120 Connecticut Ave. N.W., Suite 900
Washington, DC 20036
202-857-0166

Refuges and Wildlife
U.S. Fish and Wildlife Service
1849 C St. N.W.
Washington, DC 20240
703-358-1769

Rocky Mountain Elk Foundation
P.O. Box 8249
Missoula, MT 59807-8249
406-523-4500

Sierra Club
730 Polk St.
San Francisco, CA 94109
415-776-2211

Volunteer Opportunities for Birders
American Birding Association
P.O. Box 6599
Colorado Springs, CO 80934
719-578-9703

The Wilderness Society
900 17th St. N.W.
Washington, DC 20006-2596
202-833-2300

Wildlife Conservation Society
185th Street & Southern Boulevard
Bronx, NY 10460
718-220-5197

Wildlife Preservation Trust International
3400 West Girard Ave.
Philadelphia, PA 19104-1196
215-222-3636

World Wildlife Fund
1250 24th St. N.W., Suite 400
Washington, DC 20037
202-293-4800